*"Although there has been much touting of recent regulatory reforms, Gunther Karger's new book documents that it is still not a level playing field for the individual investor. Karger follows the money to help investors recognize the considerable dangers of fraud, corruption and unfair regulatory practice that are still thriving in our financial markets. He cuts through the deceptive Washington spin about economics and foreign policy of which there has been an abundance in recent years."*

David Rehbein, President & Chief Investment Officer
Peak Investment Management Ltd, Missoula, MT

*"If you want to know who is trying to pull one over on the American public and how they are doing it, read Gunther Karger's " Wall Street and Government Fraud". It provides clear insights into business chicanery, regulatory ineptitude and political doubletalk."*

Kevin Gale, Editor, South Florida Business Journal

*"A lot of us have the vague notion that we're being ripped off every day by Wall Street low-lifes and government politicians. Gunther Karger's book vaporizes that vague notion, replacing it with the hard facts of the scams that surround us. "You will never place your faith or trust blindly in either Wall Street or Washington after reading Gunther Karger's new book on Wall Street and Government Fraud. If you care about where your money and your votes are invested, this is a must read."*

Dan Cook, investigative journalist
Former editor of The Portland Business Journal

To: Pr Bradley - *hes*

Best wishes

5/21/08

*"My son, let them not depart from your eyes. Keep sound wisdom and discretion. Then, you will walk safely in your way and your foot will not stumble"*

The Holy Bible - Proverbs

*"The important thing is not to stop questioning."*

Albert Einstein

*"When money speaks, truth keeps silent"*

Russian Proverb

*"Judge me not by what I say, but by what I do"*

Gunther Karger

How they deceive us

# The Truth About

# Wall Street
## and
# Government

# *FRAUD*

*********************************
# Gunther Karger
*********************************

## Author of
# *Thieves on Wall Street*
### *"When money speaks, truth keeps silent"*

**Published by Discovery Group**
**Palmetto Bay, Florida**

# Wall Street and Government Fraud
## Copyright © 2005 by Gunther Karger

Cover and book design by Gunther and Shirley Karger

Published and printed in the United States by
**Discovery Group**
Palmetto Bay, Florida

**ISBN: 0-9645979-3-4**

For inquiries, contact Gunther Karger
14950 SW 86th Avenue, Palmetto Bay, FL 33158
**e-mail:** Gunther@ieee.org

*"As we set sail on our journey,
We must know wind and current,
before we can reach distant shore.*

*We must prepare for storm and
be vigilant against serpent and pirate.*

*We must set our destination
and know when we have arrived
to enjoy the harvest from our
crossing."*

**Gunther Karger – 2005**

# Acknowledgements

This book would not have been possible without the help of my editor, Shirley Karger who also is my wife. She meticulously went over each chapter as it was written and then the final manuscript. Shirley had many good suggestions and was a better error checker than the computer programs. She remembered her experience as a apprentice reporter for the New Orleans Times Picayune Newspaper.

I would be remiss in not thanking David Rehbein, my friend and former client in Missoula Montana who encouraged me to write this book. David is President of Peak Investments which advises the insurance industry. I also thank Dan Cook, investigative reporter, former editor of the Portland Business Journal and reporter for Business Week for his encouragement. I met Dan ten years ago when he discovered *"Thieves on Wall Street"* and wrote me up with a picture and a front page cover story in the Miami Business Review. We collaborated on several major corporate scandals over the years.

Finally, I must acknowledge Albert Hanser as one of the most ethical and honest corporate executives I have met along the way who also encouraged me in this project. He is CEO of Sanibel Captiva Trust Company, member of the board of the Cleveland Clinic and has served on many boards, officer of brokerage firms and corporations as well as partner in the family ownership of the St. Louis Cardinal baseball team. He also is our friend.

# Dedication

I dedicate this book to all investors who deserve better and a fairer shake. After all, it's their hard earned money which goes into the big deals we all hear about.

I also dedicate this book to **Shirley,** my wife of 51 years who stood by me and worked along my side for all those years through think and thin. Shirley, being the strong salesperson she is, compensated the "engineer and analyst" I am which helped bring to market whatever I did over the years.

I must also dedicate this book, as I do all major works, **to my parents**, Herbert and Ida Karger without whose heroic personal sacrifice I would not likely be alive today. When I was six years old, they put me on a train out of Germany to escape the fate they and my grandparents met, brutal death in the Nazi concentration camps during World War II and the Holocaust. It is in their memory I have worked over the years bringing truth to investors and when the opportunity arises, right a few of the wrongs so often seen in the financial world.

Finally, I dedicate this book **to America**, the great country which gave me a new home, opportunity and the freedom to express my views freely without fear of reprisal.

*Gunther Karger*
October, 2005

# Personal Message from Gunther Karger

## October, 2005

My parents sent me to Sweden in 1939 as part of the *"last shipment of children"* out of Germany. I was only six years old. Surviving seven years in Swedish foster homes and orphanages I was sent in 1946 to the United States as a war orphan to live in yet more foster homes until the age of 18 when I joined the Air Force and America's society. My entire immediate family had perished in the Holocaust and I faced a new life on my own. I learned that America offered great opportunity and personal freedom. Through hard work, extraordinary flexibility and the support of Shirley, my wife of 51 years, we have come to this point.

**While I still believe America is great, it has become infected with greed to unacceptable levels for the world class country the world looks to for leadership.** Although greed is inherent in human nature and will always be a part of civilization, there are thresholds beyond which it should not be allowed to cross. If it crosses over, greed becomes crime and that should not be tolerated. I believe the United States has become infected with greed to a level at which the people must act to restore its leadership to acceptable levels. This concerns CEO's of corporations as well as elected and appointed government officials who control our lives by their actions of authority.

The CEO of a company must be held accountable to employees, shareholders and customers just as our president and all elected officials must be held accountable to the citizens who elect them and in whose trust they serve.

Laws alone cannot achieve an acceptable level of greed control and honesty among corporate and government officials. Just as laws do not eliminate crimes such as murder, stealing and economic fraud, advances in technology contribute to society while also enriching the criminal's tool chest. Human nature is ingrained within us and laws only slow down crime and dishonesty the penalties rise. **The best defense in controlling these inherent problems within our society is knowledge about how our system works**. The more we know about what we are doing and the people we rely on for our lives, the better chance we have in surviving and maybe, we can even thrive personally, socially and financially in spite of all that is.

Ten years ago, I wrote the book *Thieves on Wall Street* because Wall Street became infested with financial vermins to unacceptable levels. Although some of the biggest crimes were exposed and a few people were sent to jail for a short time, **the underlying problems remained**. In this book, I told people involved with stocks how the system really works so that we all can better work within the system as it is. If we can't get rid of the crooks, then at least we can see more of them coming before they clean out our wallets. That book is as valid today as it was ten years ago and indeed was prophetic.

In recent years and still today, I see fraud and dishonesty surfacing to unacceptable levels in **business and government.** Yes, some corporate heads have rolled such as at Enron and Worldcom and the jail sentences have become much longer than in the past. However, there is plenty of fraud we don't hear much about. Beyond fraud, there is **deception which is even worse because it's much harder to detect and extremely difficult to prosecute.**

We must also recognize that elected government officials more often than before continue using their offices more for personal gain than serving the people. This is called **"self serving"** which has risen to unacceptable high levels in recent years.

The War in Iraq, how we fight terrorism, the sky high price of oil and the lack of preparedness against such world class disasters as Hurricane Katrina which nearly destroyed New Orleans are examples of ineptness and self dealing by high government officials.

Regardless of how we feel about politics, we all should know more about what's happening and how the system works. When we are told about the economy growing robustly while the federal deficit is at historic high levels and too many people still looking for work while jobs flow overseas, we need to know how to better evaluate the economic status of our country and what we are told. When we go to war and later have to hunt for reasons why we did it while thousands of people are killed and an entire country is plunged into civil war, **we need to better understand the realities of how our leaders are governing us.** When the price of oil and gasoline doubles in a year hitting deep into our pockets, bankrupting our airline industry and really hurting businesses depending on transportation, we need to be armed with the knowledge which helps us sort out fact from propaganda created by the self serving interests.

I wrote this book telling how we are being deceived and the truth you need to know about Wall Street, corporate leaders and our government. **Knowing more about this can help us better survive and even thrive.** We can't legislate morality and honesty. We can however limit the impact of people committing fraud and deception in business and government by better knowing how our financial system works and our government leaders behave.

# Content

# Why Did I Write This Book?

It's about fraud, deceit and manipulation by corporate executives and government officials, how it affects us personally and what we can do about it as individuals and together as a nation. Since business and government practices vary widely from country to country, we'll focus on what's happening right here in the United States. However, the United States is a major economic force in the world and what happens here has tremendous impact everywhere. Therefore, the ethics of how business is conducted and government behaves in the United States is becoming more crucial as the years roll on.

This book is a lot about what you don't see in the headlines. What **"they"** don't want you to know and try their best to hide is the central focus of this book. We mostly hear about the well publicized criminal business scandals but rarely about how the rest raid your wallet and get away with it. While you blame yourself, they laugh all the way to their bank with the money that once **was yours.** Unfortunately, most of them get away with it. That's how it is in business and not just in the United States. It's worldwide because it's human nature.

Knowing how the system works helps us to work within it and avoid getting caught up into its shortcomings. I wrote **Thieves on Wall Street** 10 years ago to help you better understand how the brokerage system works. In this new book, what I tell helps you put a  lock on your wallet before they get inside it.

We'll discuss how government policy is influenced by business self interests and touch on foreign policy. Is it possible that private business interests could have had a major role leading our country toward the Iraq War and even surpassed the impact of terrorism triggered by 9/11? I say yes without hesitation. We'll focus on oil as a major instrument of seeking enormous economic benefits to a few at the expense of the many.

**Can the economy be manipulated?** Again yes, and this is not a new phenomenon. I addressed it in *"Thieves on Wall Street"* which I wrote ten years ago. Today, manipulation continues on a much larger scale driven by catalysts such as greed, terrorism and ideology.

But corporations and governments don't manipulate anything. **Individuals do**. Presidents of corporations today make hundreds of millions in total compensation. The number of billionaires has swelled to nearly 500 with assets in 2004 totaling about $2.2 trillion Dollars.

Individuals including the president of the United States along with a close group of personal friends control much in the world. Do they manipulate what they control to their advantage? They have the opportunity, the power and the means to do so. **The judge of that is you!**

As in all my writings, I present herein what can be done to detect the problems addressed and how we as individuals can react to better protect ourselves. We should not assume that greed, deception and just plain dishonesty can be erased. **Our best defense is to improve our understanding of how the system works thus allowing us to work through or around it.**

*"The plans of the diligent lead to profit*
*as surely as haste leads to poverty"*
The Holy Bible, Proverbs

# Preface

This year, 2005, is the tenth anniversary of my book 'Thieves on Wall Street" wherein I told the truth about what was happening then on "Wall Street". Unfortunately, much of what I exposed in "Thieves" is still happening and that book remains valid today. Fortunately, as a result of that book and the many lectures, columns written and personal action I initiated, people became warned about the "Truths of the Street". Some likely even saved themselves from being sucked up by the schemes I exposed.

Along came Eliot Spitzer, the New York State Attorney General who dared challenge the titans of Wall Street. He accomplished much to clean up the mess which the U.S. Government's SEC failed to do. For that, I nominate Eliot Spitzer to Wall Street sainthood. He deserves that far more than the $135 million pay Dick Grasso paid himself as the Chairman of the New York Stock Exchange before he was fired for greed extraordinaire after being exposed by Spitzer.

Why write this "sequel"? It's time to do with the corporate sector what we did in 'Thieves" with the financial services business. It's time to tell the truth about what greedy corporate leaders do to pluck our pockets. Yes, I am speaking of shareholders and that's you and I.

It's once again time to tell you what they don't want you to know because this knowledge helps us survive the occasional stormy financial waters and makes life just a little harder for the financial crooks.

We are the ones who put our hard earned money to work by investing into businesses run by people we thought we could trust. We have seen industry titans routinely visit the White House to advise our president and his inner circle on what's good for America later to learn they are among the worst and least trustworthy of all.

Kenneth Lay who headed **Enron** which represented the pinnacle of corporate success and trustworthiness was among such persons. He was a frequent visitor to the White House advising our leaders on energy policy. Bernie Ebbers is another example of greed reaching the highest mountain top of corporate greed. He built Worldcom into one of the world's largest telecom business by acquiring solid companies like MCI which pioneered competition in the telecom industry. But he built his company on a foundation which crumbled when the corporate earthquake called "cooking the books" hit followed by the **tsunami called "Eliot Spitzer"**. Persons such as these are the ones who used "other people's money" to line their own pockets. Yes, I am talking about our money, yours and mine.

**Does our government have a major role in telling the truth about what's happening?** You bet! Rest assured that I will address the relationship our government plays as partners of industry to jointly "rake" in money and power sucking that right out of our pockets and lives. This role has dramatically expanded during George Bush's administration.

**Right up front and now**, I must tell you that we, Shirley and I, were solid conservative Republicans for 40 years having actively supported Republican Congressmen and Governors. We remain believers in conservative policy but not the approach taken by the Bush administration. We are not liberals just because we felt necessary to leave the GOP and as of this writing, mid 2005,    we both feel that the Democratic Party remains a party in search of a policy mainstream America needs.

**What will we discuss in this book?** Like we did in "**Thieves**", we will examine the details of what's been happening in corporate America in partnership with our government. Consider me talking with you personally, just as I do at our seminars on cruise ships, universities and private groups. If you have questions or wish to make comments, unfortunately Shirley can't spring out of this page like "Geenie" to hand you the microphone. But our email address is given elsewhere in this book and we can "speak" via this new communications means that has changed so many lives.

**The book covers** in simple words how corporate CEO's take their companies private using federal bankruptcy courts as a tool to wipe out the public shareholders. This is a rising problem stemming from the recent new federal law called '**Sarbanes Oxley**" which was supposed to fix the accounting problem, surfaced by the mega Enron and Worldcom scandals. The unintended side effect unfortunately became an enormous financial burden on companies which are required to comply with the new accounting rules. This led a rising number of smaller and marginal public companies into bankruptcy wiping out its shareholders by going private.

**We will go back to the beginning** to tell the story of Carlo Ponzi and how he developed the "**Ponzi Scheme**". We need to know about Ponzi because that's just what Enron, Worldcom and others adopted to fleece us, the public. **A little history of this** and a few others including the Tino de Angelis salad oil swindle and Barry Minkow (ZZZ Best wunderkind) gives context to the continuing evolution of corporate fraud.

I will include chapters telling about real cases I personally have been involved with and "*houses* " I helped clean. It's the old story which just won't go away and reflect that old Russian proverb "**When money speaks, truth keeps silent**".

We'll address the massive problem created out of the complex situation arising out of our **new foreign policy**, the Iraq War and the resulting impact the dramatic oil price increases have had on our economy. All this has a continuing impact on the shrinking value of the Dollar which no longer is "**king of world currencies**". Yes, we'll also discuss the increasing "**offshoring**" of much of our business. We will even address the **myths about China.** Rest assured that we will not neglect the massive problems rising in the health care industry which has been the target of a massive combined onslaught by a combination of insurance industry and government. The recently enacted Medicare Prescription Program is a good example how to manipulate an industry into ripping life savings out of our seniors pockets with the blessing of a righteous government.

As we did in "**Thieves**" we discuss **how to reform the system,** fix the problems and put us on careful personal guard against these practices. For example, I present specific corporate reforms which if implemented would put the board of directors in the position of effectively representing the shareholders. I present reforms in the health care industry combining technology and practices to make health care more affordable to most Americans with the bonus of improving the quality of that health care.

I retain the word "***FRAUD"*** as that's in the book's title and you'll find references and inferences throughout just as was found in "***Thieves***". There are two kinds of fraud. First there of course is **criminal** fraud and some of what we cover falls in that basket. Some people get indicted, some get convicted and serve jail time. But that's only the **tip of the iceberg.**

"**Wall Street and Government Fraud**" goes far beyond the criminal area reaching the "**stealth** " level. We must be able to deal with "stealth fraud" which is invisible until it hits with devastating impact. I use the term '**Stealth**" because this is like the **stealth bomber** which has been designed to be nearly invisible to radars and thus can swoop down on targets before the attacked even have the chance to defend themselves. But it gets worse. Some of the "attackers" of our wallets and personal lives succeed in emptying our wallets and ruining our lives making us believe that it's our ignorance or stupidity thus causing us to blame ourselves. That's the worst of all attacks because "they" came, stole, ruined and walked away and we didn't even know it was the result of a well planned and executed "**raid**" on our personal lives.

**I address the role of our government** and in particular, how the present administration appears to have become a partner with business in deceiving us. The book includes an entire section on the reality and truth about the U.S. economy reflecting foreign policy, the war on terrorism, Iraq and oil which is being manipulated subject to self serving interests. We all need to know the reality of the evolving global economy so we can **better interpret what we are told by our national experts and government leaders.** This reality check can help us better understand what's happening, the direction we are headed and make better financial decisions in our personal lives and for our businesses. I cover this area extensively to help us cut through the propaganda our politicians increasingly are throwing at us.

While that's probably not fraud, it often is at least deceptive and misleads us in reaching wrong conclusions. We especially need this perspective to increase our confidence in investing our money in public companies and making sound business decisions.

The book gives a **prescription for change** . I outline specific reforms needed to make our system better. Reforming how publicly held corporations should be overseen by the board of directors, changing corporate bankruptcy laws to respect the real owners of companies and fixing the health system are chapters you'll not want to miss. Our best personal defense is to continually keep vigil on our leaders and increase our understanding about how they try to steal our money and invade our lives.

*"Time is the wisest of all counselors"*
Plutarch

*"Nothing in life is to be feared,
It is only to be understood"*
Marie Curie

# How I Got Interested In Corporate Fraud

**It was 1961 and I was a young engineer only 28 years old** working for a small telecommunications consulting company in Northern New Jersey, the hot bed of the world's telecommunications research. I had already worked for Bell Telephone Laboratories and ITT laboratories where I participated in developing the world's first communications satellite. Northern New Jersey was then like Silicon Valley is today. My current assignment was to prepare a telecommunications expansion plan for a electric utility company in Venezuela so that company could get a loan from the World Bank. As an aside, one of my associates, fellow engineer and good friend was Fred Westheimer whose wife, Ruth is none other than the famous **"Dr. Ruth"**.

One day, the phone rang. It was from the Bulova Corp. which in those days was involved with much more than watches. Bulova wanted to acquire a small electronics firm making marine communications equipment. The caller asked if we *could* **evaluate the company and its products to ensure it would be a viable acquisition."** Being the adventurer already, I said we probably could but needed to check with my boss, Victor, who was the president of the company. Victor thought it would be an interesting expansion of the company's business and told me to call Bulova back telling them that we could do it and that I am assigned to the project. "Wait a minute", I said to Victor. "What do I know about mergers and acquisitions? I am an engineer". Victor said *"you can do it because you look for things most people don't and find what's in the dark corners"*. I called the Bulova guy back and accepted the assignment.

First, I checked out the company to be acquired and drove to its Long Island office. I intentionally didn't call first to make an appointment because I had remembered from my Air Force days that General LeMay of the Strategic air command often made surprise visits to bases to check to see what was really happening. And so, I arrived at an old warehouse with nothing on the first floor. Upstairs, I found some old marine communications receivers and what looked like a shut down production line. There was nobody there. But I got leads as to the origin of the company from some papers still laying around which gave me clues to what the operation was all about.

After getting back to my office in New Jersey, I checked out the ownership of this company and its history. **I struck "gold".** The company was owned by a relative of one of the Bulova board members who had made a deal to sell the business to Bulova. **The problem was that there was nothing of value to sell.**

It struck me like lightning. Why would a large multi billion Dollar corporation call a small telecom consulting company to "validate" this acquisition? The answer was that the guy calling me just needed a report "blessing" the acquisition using this report as the appraisal justifying the acquisition price to get it quickly passed by the Bulova board. He thought that a guy like me would just take the information he gave and put that into a report on our company letterhead thus rendering him an "independent report" confirming what he already had told the board.

**What did I do?** I prepared the "consultant's report" which told the truth. I simply reported therein that the **company** was a "loft operation" with outdated inventory, no operations, nil revenues and basically worthless except possibly for the value of the unexpired lease of the second floor of an otherwise empty old warehouse.

I took this to the boss who said "**I dare you to send this report out but will let you do what you think is right**." I sent the report to the client and holy hell broke out. My phone rings with the Bulova guy chewing my ass out yelling like crazy "how dare you question my information? Your assignment was to write the report verifying what I had told you". I remember telling him "**But I told you the truth** and that's what you had agreed to pay our company to find out so Bulova would have the proper information". He said "Like hell you will be paid". I responded " watch me getting paid. If your company doesn't pay the bill for services rendered and we did render the service, I will be fired and I'll do whatever it takes to prevent that."

I sent a letter with the report attached to the president of Bulova giving that company 10 days to pay the bill or I would turn our report over to the proper authorities. We got paid, I got to keep my job, Boluva didn't acquire the company, the guy who called me was fired **and I learned something I have never forgotten since.**

## *"When Money speaks, truth keeps silent"*

# Thieves on Wall Street
# 10<sup>th</sup> Anniversary

When the "**Thieves on Wall Street**" roamed on Wall Street ten years ago, we heard about wild swings in the market caused by program trading, stocks destroyed by bear raids, missing consensus and much more. We remember Michael Mllken, the junk bond king who paid over $500 million in fines but came out of jail a few years later with almost one billion still left waiting for him.

We discovered Nick Leeson who at the tender age of just 28 broke Barings Bank when he lost over $2 billion of the bank's money using the bank's Singapore office to speculate on the Tokyo Exchange. Lest you forgot, Barings was the bank the British royal family banked for 250 years and the Dutch ING insurance conglomerate bought for $1 plus the bank's debts. We mentioned Federal Reserve Chairman *Greenspan* being a master manipulator of the markets with his comments on interest rates and such likes. We focused on the brokerages and all the schemes then going on like charging excess commissions via wide spreads. I had a whole chapter on the Pink Sheets and what to do when the penny stock broker calls.

I wrote "**Thieves on Wall Street**" ten years ago and today, it is as valid as it was then. The "deals" like Worldcom just are bigger at $10 billion plus in the "cooking the book" oven with its CEO, Bernie Ebbers sentenced to 25 years instead of the few years and "slap on the wrist" we used to hear about.

The brokers play the same games. They just get bigger, more high tech and complex. Take *"program trading"* for example. This is the system used by the brokerage and institutions to trade huge volumes of stocks using mathematical models executed on ultra high speed computers. Program trading cares nothing about the investment values of the stocks bought and sold. Millions of Dollars of stock may be bought and sold within minutes causing dramatic volatility in the stock market indexes such as the NYSE. It was not uncommon for the NYSE to open up minus 25 points and close up 25 just at the end of the day often driven by these computer trading programs.

The **Crash of 1987** was in part blamed for such techniques which triggered that dramatic financial upheaval causing people to be wiped out in margin calls in a frenzied selling climax. It was estimated that during that historic market episode, program trading accounted for 17% of the daily NYSE volume. Ten years ago in *Thieves on Wall Street*, I talked about a PhD in mathematics who, along with three mathematicians used a computer to trade about 3% of the daily NYSE volume and they were funded by a Swiss insurance company. The Congress held hearings trying to outlaw such portfolio wrecking techniques which racked up huge extra income for the brokerage firms facilitating these mega transactions.

**Today, summer of 2005, program trading reaches as high as 62%** of the NYSE's total trading volume, up from the 17% it was during the 87 Crash. One day, the market opened up down minus 175 points scaring people into selling as they watched TV commentators give near hysterical explanations. Then it rose  during the day closing  up 40 points. Most major brokerage firms such as Merrill Lynch, Goldman Sachs and Bank of America routinely engage in these programs and salivate as they are hugely profitable. Think about it. You don't even need a broker or any humans to handle the trades. Just a computer and a program. It's hands off, automatic and high tech.

In "**Thieves**", I talked about banks putting people into mutual funds owned by the very same banks and not necessarily the best managed funds. I had a whole chapter devoted to financial planners steering clients into high commission funds and non liquid limited partnerships. Now, ten years later, Eliot Spitzer, the State of New York Attorney General, went after mutual fund managers who traded their own funds after market close using your money lining their pockets. After he finished off that scheme, he went onto the insurance industry where large insurance brokers sold policies not necessarily based on them being best for their clients, but based on the most bonuses paid by the insurance carriers. The largest broker, March McLennan got caught in this scheme illustrating the pinnacle of *conflict of interest.*

Ten years ago, I went into great detail about multiple broker schemes including just plain mishandling customer accounts where the client allowed discretionary accounts. Today, we hear about brokers and money managers using client money for their cars, paying for expensive trips and it has gone into the hundreds of millions.

Despite stricter laws and regulations, Wall Street is what it is. As I described in "Thieves on Wall Street", it is a **financial flea market** where any huckster can sell whatever any sucker is willing to buy thinking it's a bargain. The biggest change is that the scams get bigger, more high tech and harder to detect. How could anyone possibly have imagined that the very person routinely invited to advise the White House on energy could turn out to head one of the biggest energy scandals and corporate meltdowns in history? How is this fundamentally so different from Michael Milken walking into a large auditorium as **"king of bonds"** 20 years ago to later go on a vacation in jail for breaking securities laws?

Do you remember Spiro Agnew? I bet most people don't. He was the Vice President of the United States 1969-1973 who resigned because he was indicted for receiving kickbacks from contractors and for committing tax fraud while Governor of Maryland and Vice President. That was an example of **"The king today and dirt tomorrow"**. Not much different from Bernie Ebbers who went from telecom king to being sentenced to 25 years for cooking the books at Worldcom. As of this writing, it is questionable whether good ole Bernie will ever see jail. The Judge allowed him to be out on bail pending his appeal which could take at least a year.

Today, we hear about paying a $100 million non refundable deposit to an arms dealer for $300 million in military equipment for our war in Iraq. But when the Iraq inspectors went to Poland to check out the equipment before taking actual delivery, they found 24 outdated 30 year old Soviet era helicopters. The inspectors walked away from the deal leaving behind the $100 million deposit. Where did some of the deposit go? Some went in kickbacks to administrators in Iraq set up by the U.S.

Who paid for that? **We, the U.S. taxpayers** as part of the $200 billion price tag for that war which is raging worse than ever as I write this book. This is an example of government and private individuals joining hands in fraud against the people and that's you and I.

**So what's really changed** during the decade since I dared publish a book titled '**Thieves on Wall Street"**? In principle, not much. The fraud has just gotten bigger, more high tech and perpetrated by more respected people within America's upper crust. Today as in the late 80's, we are going once again through a period of cleansing walking former titans down their final path toward their cross. But, watching them are young disciples who will study their techniques to someday emerge to present our financial world with even bigger and much more complex fraudulent deals.

That's human nature and proven by examples referring to the chapters *From Troy to Enron* and *Ponzi's Disciples*.

*"When money Speaks, truth keeps silent"*

**and**

*"An Egg Thief becomes a camel thief"*

These quotes from Russian and Persian proverbs are as valid today as they were ten years ago when I presented them in *Thieves on Wall Street*. I suspect they will remain valid through eternity as long as human nature as we know it exists.

As I also stated in my first book to which this is the sequel, the best defense against these problems is a better knowledge of the prevailing systems and practices in place during our brief tenure in this world. That's why I wrote Thieves on Wall Street and why I now have written this book. To help us better understand how things work, the reality of our financial world and how to not only survive within it, **but possibly even thrive.**

# Fraud & Deception
# A Bit of History

*"**Fellow citizens, we cannot escape history**"*
**Abraham Lincoln**

In this section, I will discuss the history of fraud and deception going all the way back to ancient Greece and Troy 3500 years ago. We'll define truth, lies, manipulation, find out all about **Ponzi a**nd his disciples. We will examine the difference between greed and need but learn that the sentence is the same if a person is convicted. I have included the final chapter of Eastern Airlines telling the real story behind its demise and there, I tell the story as a former insider.

# Is It Truth or Lies?

**Webster says** that **truth** is a statement of fact while a **lie** is a statement which misleads or deceives.

**Gunther's definition**: **Truth** is telling what it is while **lying** is intentionally telling something you know isn't **entirely** so so.

So what's a **half lie or half truth?** It's worse than a full lie because there may be enough truth in the statement to make the rest more believable thus making it more dangerous. When a witness makes a statement under oath, that person must "tell the whole truth and nothing but the truth" or face possible perjury charges which is a criminal offense.

What about truth or lies in business? This is where that old Russian proverb explains it all "***When money speaks, truth keeps silent***". What this means simply is that when money is at stake, do a great deal of "due diligence" which means in the brokerage industry to investigate thoroughly and don't "close" on the deal or fork up your money until you feel you know enough to put your own hard money on the table.

There is an old expression "**Truth hurts**". You walk away from it afraid of hearing what it is but keep hoping it isn't so. Don't fall for this trap. Aggressively seek out the facts before you dive into a project, investment or business relationship. **Be afraid of being afraid** of not learning the truth.

It's often tough to decide whether you are being told the truth or if the person is leaving out something which could make the difference between you going ahead or walking away from it. In this case, trust the person's track record of doing what he says he'll do rather than what he promises to do. When **in doubt, trust the track record**.

**The definition of a politician** is a person who tells you what he thinks you want to hear and promises to give you whatever it takes to get your vote. Then, after he gets your vote and he is elected, all those things you heard so often fade into oblivion rarely ever to be heard again. Why is this so common with politicians? We'll add the word "*power*" to that old Russian proverb "*When money and power speaks, truth keeps silent*". Power turns on women, brings submission to your wants and ultimately leads to more money.

Do you remember the promise by a former president during his election campaign "**Read my lips**". No more taxes and then came more taxes?. A newly elected Senator issues a memo to the press on poor "Terri Schiavo" while introducing the bill into the Senate trying to get a tube back into this unfortunate person in a vegetative state for 15 years. The memo says this case is glory for the religious right's cause. But when all the politicians lose and the Judges win on behalf of this poor human being and people raise questions about that memo, the senator says "**What memo**?" and fires the aide who allegedly wrote it. President Nixon said "**What tapes?**" during Watergate times while Clinton said "**Monica who?** During Reagan's era we struggled with who knew what about the **Contra Affair** which became a football being tossed about Congress for months.

Today, the question has already faded out about the **Weapons of mass destruction no one could find** in Iraq. This is despite having sent 150,000 troops to get rid of them and a dictator which cost us taxpayers $300 billion plus thousands of lives. That's politicians and lest we forget, it's politicians **who try to tell us** how we should live and control our lives.

*Yes, truth too often fades out*
*when money and power speaks!!!*

# What is Fraud and Deception?

As in my book "**Thieves on Wall Street**" henceforth to be referred to as **"Thieves"**, I defined important terms and words as they appear. This helps gaining a common understanding and reduces misinterpretation. Let's get right to the meat of this book which is about **fraud and deception.**

**Fraud:** intentional perversion of truth in order to induce another to part with something of value or to surrender a legal right

**Deception**: an act of deceiving or misrepresenting; steering you the wrong way

The keyword here is **"intent".** Although the impact of someone intentionally lying or deceiving us can be devastating, the consequence of a **mistake** can be just as disastrous or even worse. Still, It's critically important to know the difference between someone intentionally hurting us by intent or mistake. **That difference can have dramatic legal implications.** For example, if you take a hammer and bash someone's head leading to serious injury, you face criminal assault charges and likely go to jail. But if you are on a roof and accidentally drop your hammer which then falls on a person's head, the injury could be just as serious. That's called an accident. You didn't plan it or did it out of spontaneous anger and don't go to jail.

The same principle applies to business. If you develop a plan to hide the truth leading investors to buy your stock and the investors loose their shirts when the truth unfolds, that's defrauding your shareholders by intent and subject to criminal penalties.

However, if you make a mistake in how you run your business and shareholders lose the same amount of money, that's mismanagement and negligence. You could be sued in civil court for damages.

If a doctor makes a mistake in surgery and your wife dies, that's negligence and subject to being sued for medical malpractice. If it can be proven that the doctor had a motive in killing your wife and she dies in surgery, he could face murder charges. If Kenneth Lay of Enron can prove that he didn't know what was happening with his company, he will get off free because **intent to defraud** could not be proven. He just would appear incompetent. However, if the jury decides that he as CEO of the company must have know about his company's finances and **intentionally** defrauded investors and employees, he gets convicted of fraud. **Intent** is critically important in the determination of fraud.

If things don't seem right, how can you tell if someone you are dealing with may be intentionally trying to defraud or deceive you or is he just incompetent? The first action to take if you are about to enter a business relationship is to stop it dead in its tracks. Don't go further into the deal until you further evaluate the situation and learn a lot more about the "other party". Find out what he has to gain from the "deal" and how you could loose if he gains. Remember *"When money speaks, truth keeps silent"*. We should add the word "**power**" because power to many people is as important as money. Since it's tough to determine if your suspicions are based on intent, incompetence or circumstances, walk away from the deal or situation. It's the safest thing to do. Better lose opportunity than lose what you have. Err on the side of safety. **Trust your first instinct.**

# Are We Being Manipulated?

**You bet we are!** Let's go to Webster for his definition to establish common ground.

**Manipulate:** To control or play upon by artful, unfair, or insidious means to serve one's advantage or purpose; Dealing in a security to create a false appearance of active trading, in order to bring in more traders.

Manipulation is part of our fabric of life. It's everywhere from the White House through corporate CEO's down to the fellow worker sitting in the next office trying to get your job or make out with your wife. People tell us what we will react to in a way benefiting their purpose. A presidential candidate tells the evangelists "I believe" and they vote for their "believer" based on faith **regardless of issues** relating to economy, war and foreign policy.

Arab oil ministers talk about demand outstripping supplies and the futures traders in Chicago raise oil prices putting billions of new money into their pockets as we pay the price at the pump. How do we know whether they simply are cutting back on how much oil they pump or really are running out of oil? Federal Reserve Chairman Greenspan keeps interest rates unusually low until the election but then miraculously, right after the president was appointed to another term his Federal Reserve Board changes policy leading to higher interest rates. That helped get the votes.

Kenneth Lay, CEO of Enron tells his workers that Enron is strong and growing into an even greater world energy powerhouse. He encourages shareholders and employees to buy more stock while he sells cashing in millions just before the tower of Enron tumbles as quickly as a house of cards.

A creative stock trader "going short" Johnson and Johnson stock just before he laced a few bottles of Tylenol with poison to see his profits soar as J&J stock tumbles eventually got caught. Your fellow worker aspiring to become the new boss whispers bad things about your boss. This leads to dissension in the office, poor performance and the eventual demise of your present boss. All these illustrate "**manipulation**". It's part of life. The best defense is to **get the facts before you react.**


*"Hateful to me, as are the gates of hell, is he who, hiding one thing in his heart, utters another."*
William Cullen Bryant

*"I'd rather believe the crook sitting on my side of the negotiating table than the negotiator on the other side facing me from the other side."*
Gunther Karger

# From Troy to Enron

**Long ago,** all the way back to **ancient Greece** about 3,200 years let's see what happened in the city of Troy. Paris, son of Priam, King of Troy had kidnapped Helen, wife of the Greek King Menelaus and took her to Troy where they were married. Menelaus demanded that Priam, return his beautiful wife. But he instead honored his son and refused. Menelaus sent an armada of ships with an army to rescue her. After failing to penetrate the fortress of Troy after nine years of war, Odessseus, the Greek warrior, devised an ingenious plan to **deceive** the Trojan King.

He told Sinon, the artist to build a giant **hollow wooden horse.** When he finished building the horse, Odesseus ordered his army to leave him with a few elite soldiers and the wooden horse behind. He and his soldiers then entered the horse leaving only Sinon the artist for the Trojans to see. The Trojans opened the city gate thinking they had outwitted the Greeks and won the war. Sinon complained to the Trojan king that the Greeks left him stranded because he thought more about art than war and offered the horse to Troy as a token of their victory.

Priam, King of Troy invited Sinon and **his horse** to partake of a victory celebration inside Troy. While the Trojan soldiers and the city were sleeping off the victory brew after days of drink and merriment, Odesseus and his hidden elite soldiers emerged from their wooden horse and opened the gate for the army which by then had quietly returned at night. Then, they slaughtered Troy's king and army to win the war that had gone on for nine years earlier.

What couldn't be done in nine years by two armies was accomplished in a matter of days with a few people. That's the lesson of the **Trojan Horse** and now you also know the story of '**Helen of Troy**".

The story of the **Trojan Horse** over three thousand years ago illustrates **deception and fraud**. No one within Troy knew what was about to happen. This was like a **stealth** bomber invisible to modern radars approaching the city launching bombs before the city dwellers knew what was coming. While the results were sudden and devastating, deception was well planned and started way before that historic night when the "**Trojan Horse**" was borne.

Today, it's the 21th Century. We experienced Enron, Worldcom and other mega deceptions culminating into devastating calamity for corporations, shareholders and employees and yes, for the country. These deceptions were well conceived high tech frauds taking months and genius to devise and execute. But they all hit with a sudden bang just like the Trojan Horse opening in the main square of Troy 1200 years before Christ was born. Billions of Dollars were lost, pensions vaporized and long term career employees went up in smoke. **Kenneth Lay**, armed with a PhD in economics having served as a naval officer frequently visited the White House as King of Enron, our nation's most revered energy giant to advise our president on energy policy. Suddenly, he became the **Darth Vader of business.**

I went to the story of Troy to illustrate that deception and fraud isn't a modern invention. Things just get more high tech and bigger. But let's not stop with Troy. Lets go even further back to the Biblical days of King David. He sent out his general to battle knowing he would probably be killed so David could "coveth" the general's wife. Another example of greed and deception. **Greed is inherent in human nature.** Our best defense is being better prepared and know more about the people we deal with and the situations facing us.

# Ponzi's Legacy

Occasionally we hear about a fraud or scam being "another **Ponzi Scheme**". I devote an entire session of a lecture series on corporate fraud to Ponzi because it helps us understand what we face over the years. **Who or what was Ponzi?**

Carlo Ponzi was born in Parma, Italy 1882 and came to the United States in 903 where he drifted from city to city doing odd jobs including dish washer and store clerk. He surfaced in Boston in 1917 where he gets a job processing foreign mail. He there discovered that a certificate for a U.S. Four Cent stamp could be bought in Spain for the equivalent of one Cent because of the differential values between the Spanish Peseta and the U.S Dollar. He figured he could make 400% profit by buying the certificates in Spain and redeeming them in the United States.

Carlo needed a solid sounding company name so in December 1919, he formed **The Securities Exchange Company (SEC).** Note this is **14 years before** the SEC (Securities and Exchange Commission) was formed in 1933 to regulate investments protecting the public from frauds. Carlo Ponzi prepared an investment offer(today called Private Placement Memorandum) promising investors 50% interest in 90 days to raise the money he needed to conduct this business. Word spread like wild fire that a $100 investment would return $50 in interest in just 90 days thus about doubling your money in 6 months and what a sure fire deal that was dealing in U.S. postage stamps.

But, Ponzi found that it just was impractical to actually do this deal because of the complexities involving exchanging U.S currency into Spanish Pesetas to buy the Certificates and then getting that converted into U.S postage stamps back in the U.S. So, instead of worrying about those operational details, he simply used the **new investment funds to pay new investors the 50% interest.** The postal authorities became skeptical about this and initiated an investigation into Ponzi's scheme. But nothing illegal could initially be proven. Then, when a Boston reporter wrote a story questioning the legitimacy of Ponzi's investment scheme because it simply sounded too good to be true, the investors got nervous. They rushed to his office demanding the return of their money. Ponzi kept his word by paying 1000 investors back their money plus the promised interest until the authorities declared him bankrupt and closed his office.

Shortly thereafter, Ponzi confessed he had a criminal record having served 20 months in a Canadian prison on forgery charges in a similar interest rate scheme. This had been followed in 1910 by a two year sentence when he got caught in Atlanta smuggling Italian illegals into the U.S..

Ponzi's Boston caper turned into a huge mess even by today's standards and became a gigantic swindle in that era. An estimated 40,000 people had invested about $15 million which equals $150 million in today's Dollars. Ponzi's only legitimate income was from a dividend he received from five shares of telephone stock. There was only $1.5 million left which took 8 years to distribute to the investors giving them back about 37 Cents on their Dollar, instead of doubling their money in 90 days. Ponzi was convicted on mail fraud and sentenced to a total of 14 years but skipped bond after filing an appeal after serving 3 ½ years.

**Was this the end of Ponzi"** Did he go back to Italy? No, he surfaced in Florida as Charles Borelli. He had discovered that Florida land was a hot commodity. Ponzi devised a scheme offering investors the opportunity to buy an acre for $16 to be subdivided into many smaller lots which could be sold separately leading to enormous profits. He forgot to mention that most of this land was underwater and worthless. This led him to Florida prison and again promptly jumped bail and headed for Texas.

But on the way to Texas, he was captured in New Orleans and sent back to Boston to serve his time. Ponzi was finally released on good behavior after serving 7 years of his 14 year term and headed back to Italy. There, he became friends with Benito Mussolini, the Italian dictator who appointed him to be the Rio de Janeiro, Brazil branch manager of a new Italian airline serving in that position from 1939-1942 far away from the ravages of the war which had erupted all over Europe. Always on the lookout of a buck via financial swindles, Ponzi discovered that several airline officials were using the airline to smuggle illegal currency. He tried to get his "cut" from that swindle but when they refused Ponzi turned them into the Brazilian authorities for a reward. This scheme coupled with the war led to the Brazilian authorities to shut down the airline and Ponzi lost the last job he would have.

Carlo Ponzi, died penniless in 1949 in a Brazilian charity hospital leaving as his personal legacy to the world an unfinished manuscript titled '*The fall of Mr. Ponzi*'. But Carlo Ponzi left a much greater legacy. He even today is famous for the **'Ponzi Scheme"** and the **"Pyramid Scheme"** which keeps cropping up here and there. Ponzi surfaced nearly all over the world over a 40 year time span. He kept going until his physical end at age 67 but lives on through his legacy.

The name **"Ponzi Scheme"** came up when Glenn Turner, the hare lipped **snake oil super salesman** used the slogan *"Dare to be great"* while giving seminars all over Florida recruiting multi level marketing people selling his snake oil derivative cosmetics. The problem was that the people were super motivated to sign up "downline" distributors for which their "upline" masters would give handsome bonuses but not much, if any **snake oil would flow through the chain**. Florida regulators declared that a pyramid scheme and passed legislation making that illegal. That was the end of Turner in Florida but alas, there was Arizona in his future.

**Enron** comes to mind as a pyramid or 'Ponzi Scheme". This resulted from the liabilities flying off the corporate balance sheet to land on offshore partnership accounting books in a Cayman Island corporation with an office no larger than a post office box which forwarded the mail right back to the Houston Enron Tower.

No doubt, Carlo Ponzi will live for a long , long time in the annals of business fraud. And that's the lesson of "Ponzi". It keeps coming back . We must always be on the vigil for financial scams so long as there is greed.

*"If it sounds too good to be true,
it probably is"*

# Ponzi's Disciples

It's said that "*once an engineer, always the engineer*". That compels me to mention an important scientific principle which still rules the universe, *The Law of Conservation of Energy*. This law states that energy may neither be created nor destroyed and that the sum of all the energies in the system is constant. It can however, be transformed from one form to another.

Now, let's transform this scientific law into business law or simply put, the law of plain truth. "**You can't get something for nothing**". If you want to cook a stew, you have to put something into the pot. This reminds me of what happened to my wife and me shortly after we were married and arrived to our new home, a windowless attic apartment in Central Illinios in the dead of the winter. She wanted to make a pot of coffee using the new electric coffee maker we got for a wedding gift. From the kitchen, Shirley yells out "*Do I have to put in water*"? I say " Do whatever you want". After a while, we started to smell burning coffee and I ask " *Honey, did you put water into the pot?*" Shirley says "*You didn't tell me to*". That was the end of the new coffee pot and proves in non scientific terms this important principle.

**What do all thieves have in common?** Laziness. They want something you have or did. They don't want to work and expend the energy required to get what they want.   They simply steal if from you who worked hard to create it. They also want it quick.

So they invent all sorts of schemes to snatch from you what you worked hard to get over many years. Some of them are smart, very smart.

**Tino de Angelis**, the son of Italian immigrants liked the food business and he was very smart. He cooked up a complex scheme involving futures contracts on salad oil. Tino took out loans using as collateral salad oil stored in huge tanks on the Jersey shore.

American Express sent inspectors(appraisers) to inspect the tanks verifying that the product actually existed in the tanks and measured the stored liquid. Since the inspectors did see vegetable oil topping off the tank, they approved the contracts and paid Tino millions.

But, what the inspectors really approved was **oil floating on top of water** which is mostly what the tanks were filled with making the contracts worthless. Tino used the scientific principle that oil floats on top of water thus hiding the water. This scheme involved a complex system of futures contracts, brokerage guarantees and investors who bought the securities this great scheme created. When it was discovered at delivery time that most of the fluid was water instead of salad oil, Tino's scheme collapsed but he already had the money. By the time this scandal was over, Tino's commodity business was bankrupt, brokerage houses folded and a subsidiary of American Express became bagholders for hundreds of millions dollars having gone up in smoke. Guess what? Tino tried to get something where there was nothing, just like good ole Carlo Ponzi did with his Postal scheme. Here is an interesting historical note. All this started to unfold when JFK was assassinated in 1963.

Let's move to the wild 80's where all sorts of **mayhem happened on Wall Street and meet Barry Minkow**, the wunderkind who at age 16 conceived the idea of a novel commercial carpet cleaning business. If he could create a publicly owned company with the respect of trading on the New York Stock Exchange, his scheme could make him millions.

The company had to be public so there could be options and here is why. He would offer office buildings multi year carpet cleaning contracts and lucrative options on stock in his company which he named **ZZZ Best.** Then, he could use these multi year contracts to project increased revenue and earnings over the next several years and that's food for a moving stock.

The options would become more valuable than getting the carpets cleaned. So Barry goes to his good friend **Michael Milken**, the Junk Bond King(we'll get to him later) who takes ZZZ Best public. By the time all this was over with the stock going nearly to the Moon and then sinking to nothing, Barry went to jail, the shareholders of ZZZ Best lost just as in later years shareholders in Enron and Worldcom lost for similar reasons. But it doesn't end there. While in prison, Barry's Mother and her friend who (I knew) was a big mover in Southern California evangelism go to pray with him and this nice Jewish boy discovers Jesus. By the time he graduates from Prison at age 24, Barry is an ordained minister and does a great job praising the Lord raising money for his ministry. I heard one of his sermons. He is real good.

Now, we remember **Michael Milken** who became known as the King of Junk Bonds and one of the main characters at a major Wall Street firm named Drexel Burnham. He was known as the person who could make the deal fly regardless of risk and that's where the term "**junk bond**" came from. The higher the risk, the higher the interest the bonds paid. What investor wouldn't invest in bonds paying 15-20% interest when the bonds were issued by a top and well known Wall Street Firm? This was in the mid 80's when the "Game on the Street" was mergers and acquisitions. Someone whispers that an acquisition was about to happen, the stock would fly and fortunes be made.

Well known people such as **Ivan Boesky,** the corporate raider and **Dennis Levine,** the Wall Street facilitator became involved with a myriad of insider trading schemes making them millions at the expense of the public shareholders who "found out the good stuff" after it was already milked by the "**inside traders**". By the time this all was rooted out by a rising star named **Rudy Giuliani** when he was U.S. Attorney for New York City, later to become its Mayor, the House of Drexel was gone, the Junk Bond King was in prison as were a few others.

Michael Milken settled for a reduced sentence by paying a record fine of about $600 million. But he also retained nearly a Billion Dollars after paying this. Not a bad payday. **Guess where all this money came from?** Commissions and fees from all those deals and that money got squeezed out from all those transactions paid for by the shareholders and investors. Folks, **that's you and me** and the rest of us. Money has to come from somewhere to comply with the "Law of Conservation of Energy" and the more common law " you can't squeeze something from nothing".

These and others should have been given diplomas from " **Ponzi College**". I touched on just a few of the birds which raided our wallets during the early days. It's good to occasionally visit history because these things keep coming back in our time as bigger and nastier schemes. I would be remiss not mentioning my first book, "*Thieves on Wall Street*" which goes into great detail about the "Process of the Street". This book tells about lots of schemes and how it happens.


"*Hope of ill gain is the beginning of loss*"
Democritus

42

# Greed or Need?

**What happened during the past five years?** For answers, we roll time back to the late 90's. The Internet revolution had triggered staggering growth in the telecom industry. The perception was that soon, everybody would be using the computer for everything imaginable. We were even told that most business would be conducted on the Internet and our primary means of communications would use the Internet. The computer and Internet became the rage of students with young people emerging as computer whiz kids.

Yes, we definitely were gearing up for the cyber age. All that meant anything would be done using computers. The Internet would connect us all to each other doing all that matters. Companies sprang up such as Global Crossings which laid high capacity cables across the oceans and continents to serve this exploding industry. The telephone companies laid out plans to handle this forever expansion of communications traffic, High tech companies sprang up like flowers in the spring time to create new and better technologies to serve this nirvanian information explosion. Yes, **Worldcom** was born on this trip toward the 21th Century.

How would this industry pay for all this growth? That was a slam dunk. The stocks of these Internet and telecom companies were rising like rockets creating massive value. Not uncommon were companies with no revenues and maybe not even products whose stocks were flying from nothing to $200 per share. Fortunes were created and the investment banks looked to make a killing on what was to happen. They funded new companies headed by kids barely out of school with no experience in running any kind of business but who had some idea of how to make even more money on this rolling money train.

Then, along the way came Alan Greenspan who told us about *"Irrational Exuberance"* which gave the market a bad case of the flu. **George Bush** arrives during the fall of 1999 presidential campaign telling us that unless he is elected, a bad recession is right around the corner. Enough business leaders believed this and started to scale back capital expansion and hiring which accelerated the economic slowdown which was mildly underway following a record long expansion during the 90's. Economic forecasts were adjusted downwards pushing the stock market over the mountain and it started rolling down from its lofty perch. This led to the avalanche we know as the **"bursting of the Internet bubble"**.

We suddenly realized that the whole world would not become a "**cyberworld**" overnight and that companies actually must have revenues and profits **within our lifetime**. This awakening also led to the realization that the telecom providers had been moving too rapidly installing broadband capacity resulting in a dramatic slowdown in equipment purchases. That dropped the next shoe which was the **telecom meltdown.** Stocks in the telecom sector crashed to earth with some even below ground to be buried in Chapter 11 or coming to final rest in Chapter 7.

Starting early in this process which took several years, corporate managers came under **intense pressure to maintain earnings and revenue growth**. As the revenue and earnings started to decline, corporate managers took creative actions to prop up their stocks. **The companies struggled to meet their financial obligations** while drastically scaling back growth plans. Their growth money had vanished in the telecom stock meltdown because they could no longer sell their stock to raise the cash needed to continue their plans. Some stocks had crashed from lofty $100 plus to penny stock below even one Dollar.

Along this slide, corporate managers had valid reasons to stem the slide of their stock including raising capital to finance their growth plans.

But they also had a strong incentive to make a killing on their stock options. **This is where the good guys got separated from the bad ones with marginal CEO's crossing over the line**. Some managers continued to be driven by need while a growing number allowed greed to rule. They applied high tech and complex methods for propping up revenues and earnings to non existent levels. The results and bottom line became unfortunately an industry disaster. Bankruptcies with thousands of employees losing jobs and careers. People started to do weird things. **Enron** and **Worldcom** happened but you should know there were many other companies **affected which you have never heard of.**

Just as the industry and the economy started to crawl back, we were **slammed by 9/11.** The airline industry was grounded with national transportation coming to a halt. The NYSE and all markets were halted for an entire week making financial history . We witnessed the official birth of the war on terrorism. Then, we struggled coming back from this disaster surviving the war in Afghanistan with the country assuming the Iraq war would also be a quick event.

**But we were wrong.** Although the "**War**" was declared won by President Bush May 1, 2003, it kept going on and on and getting worse instead of better, as of fall of 2005 when this book was written. The federal deficit mushroomed to a record nearly $500 Billion deficit driven by war spending rising to $200 billion. Adding to this economic burden came along the oil shocker of prices eventually tripling to nearly $60 per barrel by the spring of 2005 then rocketing to $70 with gasoline at $3 plus per gallon driven by Hurricane Katrina's ill wind and floods roaring into the upper Gulf oil patch.

These factors extended the economic downturn and made recovery more difficult continuing pressures on business executives struggling with flagging revenues, rising interest rates and in many cases, running out of cash.

This long term process led to even more executives to cross the line into the land of unethical if not downright illegal activities including **cooking the books.**

I address this process in detail because while there always are greedy people doing all they can to steal and swindle other peoples Dollars, the conditions of the past five years likely **created fraudulent situations out of necessity.** It's important to understand this process so we can be better equipped to detect such things during future years.

**Do you think we are finished?** Absolutely not! We would be remiss not addressing the role our government had in all this. Domestic economic policy of reducing taxes when we should conserve public funds and a foreign policy leading to a 30% Dollar devaluation resulted in disaster. The Bush Administration's approach to the **"War on Terrorism"** inclusive of the Iraq War led to loss of confidence by many foreign leaders and skyrocketing oil price stifling potential economic growth. Did you think we would forget the health care problems weighing on the economy and nation? **No way! Read on.**

# Eastern Airlines
# The Truth About It's Failure

**Remember Eastern Airlines?** This was the airline which started in 1926 carrying mail between New York and Atlanta to eventually become the second largest airline in the world with 40,000 employees and 225 airplanes serving 125 cities in the U.S., Latin America and a few in Europe. The company generated at its peak over $4 billion in revenues. Eastern was a pillar of the communities it served and especially Miami where its 13,000 employees worked at its main facilities and Hq. But it was sold in 1986 and filed for bankruptcy 1989 as a wholly owned subsidiary of Texas Air. Why did this great airline and company fail? Although books have been written about it, the straight simple truth hasn't been told publicly and in detail until you read this chapter.

**Who am I to tell this story?** I worked for the person who was responsible for Eastern's demise and I was responsible for preparing the company's forecasts. **I was on the inside witnessing the story unfold firsthand** and on several occasions, warned the local civic leaders to talk some sense to the Company's CEO who was leading a once great company into ruin.

**Why am I telling this story in this book?** Because Its about corporate fraud of the worst kind. This is **stealth fraud** committed by a person considered super good by the business, local community and employees. Rather than writing another book about Eastern Airlines and there have several, I think it deserves a chapter in this book.

The demise of Eastern Airlines has been blamed on Airline Deregulation which happened in 1979, too much debt buying the wrong airplanes and especially on the mechanics union headed up by Charlie Bryan.

But these were challenges which an experienced management team could and should have worked through resulting in the company's survival. **The real problem** was Frank Borman, the astronaut who piloted the first spacecraft to the Moon in the 60's and headed Eastern Airlines for 16 years until 1986 when he sold it to Texas Air. Borman was a great pilot and had high moral standards. But he should have remained a pilot or served some company in a technical role. The sum total of his management training and experience before taking over as CEO of Eastern in 1970 was a three month executive development program at Harvard Business School to which Eastern sent him **and paid for.** For 16 years, Borman ran Eastern on a **"wing and a prayer"**. I remember many memos from Frank which he always ended with *"May God Bless you"* while he was **winging it** on the top floor of Building 16 at the Miami International Airport in his executive office.

I remember a meeting in 1979 where we gathered around the executive conference table going over the forecasts and finances for the following quarters. Dr. Wayne Yeoman, Chief Financial Officer exclaimed with surprise when we presented the forecast "*My god, the expenses will exceed the revenues. What will we do?"* I replied "*Wayne, that's your job. You are in charge of finances."*

But how was Wayne to know how to do it? Dr. Yeoman had a doctorate in military science and was selected for the CFO job by his friend, Frank Borman because he was the Superintendent of the West Point Military Academy when Frank went there. Wayne was a great guy and nice to work with but had no background in corporate management or finance.

Then we had Jose, an industrial engineer who was the Vice President of Financial Controls promoted to that job because Frank thought it was important to have a Cuban as a vice president in the company.

Jose may have been a great industrial engineer but he was not necessarily a strong financial leader which the company needed badly. Properties and Facilities valued in the billions was headed by Frank's former Air Force friend and retired colonel. When the A300 first became available, Borman wanted Eastern to be the first U.S. airline to fly this new European built fuel efficient airplane. When we presented the forecast for that time period, I said " Since we are headed into an economic slowdown and need to reduce capital outlays, is this the time the company should borrow a billion Dollars to buy airplanes not yet needed? I got "thrown" out of the room and the aircraft were bought adding billions to an already heavy debt load.

The A300 was a wide body aircraft with space under the passenger deck for 16 cargo containers. Since cargo likes to fly at night and passengers by day, someone came up with the idea of flying the A300 at night with a hub at Houston serving primarily cargo. The idea was based on selling all the cargo space for each flight to a freight company and getting the pilots to agree to fly extra hours at night at a reduced pay rate. When the program came up for review and I did the forecast for it, I stood up and asked "*Where are the expenses for the program? The expenses must be less than revenues.*" I was told to mind my business as **Frank would take care of the pilots and the expenses.** This service named "The Moonlight Special" was launched even after Borman failed to get the pilots to agree to the reduced pay and the expenses were grossly underestimated. That poor business decision cost Eastern about $250 million in additional losses.

Borman being from Tuscon, Arizona wanted his airline to fly to his hometown. The analysis said it would be a significant money loser due to Eastern's route structure. But Frank said he "felt it was right" and Eastern flew to Tuscon until someone finally convinced him to stop that money loser.

The problem mounted as Borman sought wage concessions from the unions which became more and more resistant and aggressive against top management.

By about 1983, there was yet another strike threat because of the widening rift between unions and management. Management blamed the problems on high paid union workers and yes, they were paid too much relative to the deregulated market place. Unions blamed the problems on bad management.

**I came up with a plan whereby the company could save about $750 million** over three years which would also restore some harmony between management and unions. Instead of paying out the scheduled raises under existing union contracts, the company would issue stock in lieu of those raises thus making the employees a 20% shareholder. The theory was and remains today that people who own the company would work more harmoniously for the common good. I received tentative approval from the major unions but Borman turned it down because the plan included board representation by the employee group owning the 20% block of shares. That killed the deal and **sealed Eastern's fate**.

Borman gave the workers the ultimatum early in 1986 to either accept another 15% paycut or he would sell the airline to Texas Air and Frank Lorenzo who was hated by airline unions. The unions agreed on the condition that Borman steps down. Borman refused to give up the reins, even after 16 years of trying and failing and sold the airline to Frank Lorenzo. Borman retired by sailing into the Arizona sunset with a great golden parachute while Lorenzo installs his people who sell off Eastern's most valuable assets to Continental Airlines and finally files Chapter 11 in 1989. The court sends in Martin Shugrue to run the bankrupt Eastern trying to revive it but fails as it shuts down on its final day on January 18, 1991. Who was Martin Shugrue?

He had worked for Frank Lorenzo at Continental Airlines which went through bankruptcy, at Pan AM when it went bankrupt and actually had management experience only at airlines which at some point did file Chapter 11 or went out of business. He had lots of experience with leading companies into bankruptcy but none getting them out of it.

**There are two stories I must end with because they illustrate why the story of Eastern Airlines belongs in this book on corporate fraud**. Once, I was told to raise my revenue forecast to meet banking requirements on Eastern's debt, even though that meant artificially raising the revenues. **I refused** on the ground that was altering documents covered under federal accounting regulations and equivalent to "**cooking the books**". This would have been like putting down false assets on an application for a bank loan which is a criminal offence. My refusal probably cooked my career at Eastern

This would not have been much different than Andrew Fastow, the Enron CFO, setting up offshore partnerships hiding Enron's liabilities or the Worldom CFO transferring $11 billion of expenses to the capital side of the balance sheet. This was similar to what happened after the 2000 stock market meltdown and the companies struggling through difficult times.

As mentioned early in this book, this became a situation where some people would cross the line of ethical and criminal behavior based on a combination of **greed or need.** I would not cross that line.

**The second story** is about the financing of Texas Air's funding the takeover of Eastern Airlines. One of the banks which was raising the money was Centrust Savings & Loan of Miami, one of Miami's largest banks. The senior vice president of Planning at **Eastern Airlines** was on that bank's board of directors and chairman of its executive committee.

His wife was an art consultant to the bank's CEO getting paid well for buying the bank millions of Dollars in fine art decorating the bank's executive suite. This was a definite **conflict of interest** situation which should never have been allowed. Centrust Savings failed, was liquidated and its CEO indicted on criminal charges and served at least ten years in jail. The Eastern Airlines vice president sailed into his sunset with his golden parachute.

**What was the real problem at Eastern Airlines?** Inexperienced and very stubborn management. Yes, there were union problems. But in my opinion, that's a management responsibility to work through. As difficult as labor troubles may be to resolve, it's management's responsibility to prevent the worst of these and solving those which occur. After a few years of trying and failing, Frank Borman should have given up the CEO position to give someone else a chance to get the job done. But he didn't and the worst of all, his board allowed him to stay and supported his management decisions. **This was one of the worst board failures in modern corporate history** because it took so long to evolve and there were so many opportunities for it to address the problems. It was worse than what happened at Enron because there, the situation occurred over just a few years with the board members saying "*We didn't know.*"

The Eastern directors knew and had at least ten years to change management and failed to do it. They kept saying "**Frank knows what's best**" and left him to do whatever he wanted. Yes, Borman, Eastern's CEO knew what was best for the company. He led it right to the cliff from which fell 40,000 employees, families were destroyed, pensions were lost and more Eastern employees committed suicide than were killed in action during the Gulf War.

*"Failure is the refusal to learn from experience"*
Gunther Karger

# Corporate Fraud
# Marches On

*"There is no fire like passion, there is no shark like hatred, there is no snare like folly, there is no torrent like greed"* Buddha

We'll bring "*Thieves on Wall Street*" up to date to learn that the main thing changed is that the crooked deals got more high tech and bigger. We'll learn **that Enron was the "9/11" of corporations erupting a volcano already simmering just as existed with terrorists** . We'll see that the bankruptcy has become license to steal from shareholders and I have even included a corporate obituary signed by a coroner. We'll discover the Silicon Valley Raiders, how they manipulate forecasts and spin numbers to please your wallet leaving nothing but vacuum behind. We'll discover that class action legal suits have become the lawyer's gold train.

# The Thieves on Wall Street Are Still Going Strong

*"You have e-mail"* your computer speakers sing to you. It's a message about a company reporting to be making a $7 offer for a stock trading for 30 Cents. The story is all over the Internet bulletin boards. I happen to know the CEO of that company and called him to ask if it's for real. He laughs and says *"I wish it were"* . I watch the stock for a couple of days noticing it shoots up on high volume to about $1.50. Within a week, the stock drops right back down where it had been without any announcement. I report it as a *"Pump & Dump"* scheme to the authorities. It was traced to an 18 year old fellow in Vancouver who created the rumor, bought a bunch of shares before he spread it out all over the Internet and then dumped it when the stock rose on high volume triggered by traders who thought "something was happening" and tried to make a quick buck. But the "**quick buck**" was made by the young fellow in Canada who was later paid a visit by the Mounted Police. Eventually, he was forced to pay back the illegal profits and pay a stiff fine. That happened about 8 years ago.

Let's go to July 19, 2005 and a Wall Street Journal article which caught my eye. Many of us remember the heady 80's when legendary oil investor and corporate raider T. Boone Pickens made hundreds of millions of dollars investing in oil and gas stocks and many traders tried to anticipate what Pickens might do next to ride that wave into the golden corral. The WSJ article was not about T. Boone Pickens but about his son, Michael who had apparently tried to achieve his success taking a different path.

The 51 year old younger Pickens was arrested by federal agents charged with securities fraud for allegedly manipulating thinly traded stocks through **a pump and dump** scheme broadcasting faxes all over about stocks which were expected to triple. He had an accomplice in Florida who was also arrested. Both face up to 20 years and $5 million in fines.

Let's again go a few years back to 1998 when the SEC in cooperation with law enforcement agencies across the entire country filed 23 actions against 44 individuals who used the Internet to defraud investors all over the world in pump & dump schemes. These people used email, online newsletters, bulletin board message postings, faxes and whatever technology was then beginning to offer.

About ten years ago, I **helped the SEC nail a CEO** who had set up accounts for his children for the purpose of manipulating his own company stock. He bought stock in these accounts driving up the price while he sold out of his own account and concurrently issuing gloriously positive news from the company. Incidentally, that company eventually was liquidated as the CEO faced federal charges and eventually was convicted of securities fraud, tax evasion, money laundering and illegal use of corporate funds.

Based on what I see rolling daily into my email box and fax, the only thing I see changed is that more of the same is happening. But it's more refined, has the guise of professionalism made available by great imaging and electronic messaging. The Internet has many websites promoting stocks usually paid by the company and that's mostly legitimate investor relations promoting their companies. It's important though, that you realize that these are paid ads and thus, not necessarily very objective. They typically amplify the goodies and put the negatives in small footnotes or just refer you to the SEC filings which typically are full of doom and gloom disclosures.

Let's go to the Proxim corporate website and it's July 20, 2005. The first thing you'll see is a window in the center of your screen flashing in multi colors "**The New Proxim – stronger than ever**". "**World leader in wireless technology over 25 years**". What the investor seeing this probably didn't know is that this is a company being sold in a bankruptcy auction this very same day to the highest bidder for $28 million with over $100 million in debts. You guessed right, the shareholder gets nothing, zero, and the shares trading that day even at 5 Cents are worthless because they represent an empty shell stripped of the operating business. The company's technology and all its assets plus its operating business is being sold to another company which offered the highest bid in bankruptcy court. Of course, if you go into the inner reaches of the website to the SEC filings, you would find that the company filed for Chapter 11 on June 11, just a little over 1 month before the fire sale on the "courthouse steps".

Yes, **the Thieves are still at it.** They just keep getting smarter, get into larger "projects" and use **high** tech tools to do their thing. It's like a previous chapter titled "**From Troy to Enron**". As always has been and will continue to be, our best defense is knowing how these systems work and how we too can survive and maybe even thrive. But we must always be on the lookout for **Thieves** who have roamed since even before Robin Hood rode his stallions through Sherwood Forest to avoid the Sheriff of Nottingham.


*"He who can have patience can have what he will"*
Benjamin Franklin

# Yes, Institutions Do Commit Fraud

**Institution**: an established well known organization, society or corporation (as a college or university) especially of a public character

We associate *"institution"* with something very strong, trusting and lasting. Universities, The Supreme Court, The Congress, giant insurance companies, hospitals and banks are considered institutions. When we think of something being *"institutional"*, we think of something we can trust.

Financial services companies tend to call themselves institutions to portray a place of trust because they want us to trust them with our money. Some banks even call themselves "**trust Companies**" because they want you to entrust them managing your investments. Such companies are subject to regulations imposed by federal and state governments in addition to restrictions they place on themselves by their own industry groups. Brokerage companies have created another institution called "**investment bank**". These take private companies public by structuring the deal and assign the brokerage side of the "**house**" the task of selling the new shares to the public. Investment banks also facilitate mergers and acquisitions and occasionally participate in the deals themselves.

But, we should remember that **insane asylums** also are institutions. As we should recall the news of April 22, 2005 summarized as follows: " *A former managing director at SG Cowen & Company pleaded guilty to a charge that he shorted stock in companies that were contemplating a type of securities offering that typically results in falling share prices.*"

What is SG Cowen? SG Cowen Securities Corporation is the U.S. securities and investment banking firm owned by Societie Generale, the giant French based insurance and financial services company with 92,000 employees in 80 countries founded 150 years ago. A pillar of high respect!

SG Cowen, is considered an "*institutional investor*" since it buys and sells securities for its own account and its clients. The former managing director was based in Switzerland when he conducted **short raids** on several U.S. publicly owned companies. For that, he will face prison terms resulting from the use of this illegal insider trading scheme I call short raid.

What's a "**short raid**". You better know about it because it has been and continues to be a rampant practice by institutions and very large investors. To learn what it is, how it works and how institutions often make a killing at your expense, let's examine in detail how an institution in collusion with a U.S. public company defrauded the shareholders of this NASDAQ traded company. I will omit the names of the target company and the institution involved as this defrauding process was still under way when this was written. As in "**Thieves on Wall Street**", the focus in this book is about the process and **how it's done** so you will be better prepared the next time. I will intentionally describe a scheme in step by step detail because it illustrates a widespread practice.

This knowledge will help you detect and avoid similar situations and you should know they are widespread industry practices.   Let's call the subject company **Orion** and the institution is named **invest.**

While these are fictional names, they represent real companies and what actually happened. Orion was a high tech California based company with revenues of about $100 million and in financial difficulty. In spite of strong industry fundamentals, its financial performance had suffered for the past two years while it digested mergers and acquisitions for growth.

Early in 2005, the company announced it raised $9 million by selling 5 million shares at $1.80 per share. **Invest,** an institutional investment firm representing investors principally from the Pacific Far East. During the prior week, the shares were slipping from about $2.5 to about $1.80 on the day of the announcement. That's great, thought many Orion shareholders. If an institution invests $9 million cash at $1.80, *"that's good enough for me and I'll hold my stock and maybe even buy more to average down since I bought way over $10."*

About three months later when Orion's stock had further crashed to 70 Cents, it miraculously started to skyrocket on high volume. In just two days, it rose from 70 Cents to $1.20 but settled back to 83 Cents just three days later. This went up on my radar as something very fishy.

Interesting, the volume of shares traded during these three days above the average daily volume of the past 30 days was approximately equal to half of the 5 million shares the company sold three months earlier.

Here is the big question. **Why did the stock so suddenly rise on high volume?** There was **no good news** from the company to account for the rising stock. But there was plenty of recent bad news such as revenues significantly dropping, losses rising and its auditor even had issued a warning that the company might not make it.

Worse still, Orion's latest SEC filings warned that it could run out of cash, may have to file for bankruptcy and it likely would have to sell off significant assets to raise the cash to pay down a big loan due by midyear.

There was no reason for the stock to go up but every reason for the stock to drop further and even face delisting from the Nasdaq. Why in the world would a smart financial institution invest $9 million in Orion when it had to know all about these problems? Read on and you'll know why and how this fraud was perpetrated.

It's simple. The **institution knew** the company was in trouble and had much more information about this than the rest of the shareholders. The Chief Financial Officer knew the principal of the institutional investment banker and together, they cooked up a scheme reducing the risk of loss to the institution to almost zero while providing $9 million fresh capital to Orion. Based on the scenario on which the Swiss investment banker got convicted I will describe what likely happened in this case. Just realize that it is the same company but a more recent and different investment banker.

When the deal was agreed on and the investment banker and company had set the price and date for the offering, the institution started to **sell short** shares against the 5 million new shares they knew they would be buying. They likely sold about 2.5 million shares short at an average price of $2.25 putting $5.6 million cash into the institution's bank account. This immediately created a credit of $5.6 million against the $9 million to be paid out within a week or so to the company in the actual purchase of the 5 million shares. The result of this is a net investment cost or risk at only $3.4 million which translates to 68 Cents per share. The institution also knew that the shares would likely go down further because Orion's Board had just executed an executive compensation agreement with the CEO and Chairman to be paid an approximate $1 million bonus if they sell the company or sufficient interest therein to effect a change in control.

This bonus would be paid regardless of share price. The renewed employment contract provided for the continued near half million Dollar per year salaries for the two in the face of deteriorating company financials and reaching a cash critical stage. So, the stock continued its trek downwards until it reached a low of about 70 Cents. At that time, the institution could **cover its short position** by repurchasing the 2.5 million shares it sold short. However, if the stock tanked  due to bankruptcy which it did,  the institution would avoid this covering expense altogether.

The cost of this repurchase would have been an estimated $2.25 million resulting in a net $5.6 final cost of the investment or about $1.12 per share. However, the institution also knew via its close relationship with the company's top management that an asset sale would take place and that likely would result in a priority allocation of proceeds to certain institutional investors That would cause the final investment by the institution to be nearly zero. But what about the profit? Yes, there was a probable 6% commission in the $9 million stock transaction giving the institution an estimated half million cash. Meanwhile, the company had the $9 million additional cash to pay its key management the horrendous salary and potential bonus upon sale of the company.

**What's wrong with this scenario?** A lot! The institution bailed out a company in dire financial straights but using a scheme reducing the risk of loss to nearly zero with the help of insiders and nearly guaranteed an estimated half Million Dollar profit.

If the insiders had also strapped themselves with a stringent cost reduction program to save the company, at least the intent would have been honest. But they kept right on giving themselves way above industry norm salaries. Much worse still, they factored themselves into a million Dollar bonus for selling the company or business segments of it regardless of what this meant to the rest of the shareholders and yes, the employees.

The scheme was **immoral and unethical** as the executive team enriched itself at the expense of the shareholders many of whom lost 90% of their investment and employees who lost their jobs. **But it also was illegal** and should be subject to criminal prosecution with some going to jail or at least face stiff fines. **Why was it illegal?** Because a select outside investor conspired with insiders to structure a scheme enriching themselves at the expense of outside shareholders. **That's securities fraud.**

**What's the lesson here?** Anytime you see a company announce its intent to offer shares via a private placement or secondary registration prior to it actually happening, **watch out!** This is called a "**shelf registration**" which allows the company to offer new shares at nearly any time it pleases. You also should assume that there will be short sellers to take advantage of this to your detriment. To protect yourself, consider selling a portion of your shares or at least hedge by going short a portion of your shares as insurance. You should assume that the stock likely will go down upon such news. If in doubt, play it safe. Sell and put your investment money elsewhere. It's better to observe this from the sidelines with your cash elsewhere. You can always get back into the stock.

*"An institution can be the U.S. Supreme Court or the insane asylum"*
Gunther Karger

# Enron's legacy
# The 9/11 of Corporations

Little did we know on that fateful morning of 9/11 that just one month after the Twin Towers melted down, America would experience its **corporate meltdown** equivalent we now know as "**Enron**". While the Twin Towers standing physically tall in New York as it did in world stature crashed in a flash triggering immense personal and global economic shock, **storm clouds were gathering over the gleaming Enron tower in Houston.** As Kenneth Lay, Enron's CEO, the revered titan of industry shared his unquestioned corporate wisdom with his buddies in the White House guiding them to formulate national energy policy, little did anyone know that his **Enron empire would topple just one month after 9/11.** Like 9/11 changed the world and especially America, "Enron" changed the world of business as we knew it. We won't dwell on what happened in 'Enron". That's well chronicled elsewhere but we do refer to it often in this book.

We should know however, that as did the factors leading up to 9/11 exploding over New York and the Pentagon, there had been rumblings prior to Enron erupting as a corporate volcano. When it happened just a month after the twin towers fell in New York, its fallout spread all over America and beyond. **Enron became America's corporate 9/11.**

The fundamental factors leading up to that October 2001 corporate disaster were covered in ***Thieves on Wall Street,*** the book I wrote ten years earlier and lectured extensively on during years preceding **10/11.**

Note that I just coined a new word which should be remembered as in 9/11. It's **10/11** and stands for **October 11, 2001 when a new era in corporate America was heralded in by the "crashing tower of Enron".**

The day was October 11, 2001 when a lawyer at Enron's accounting firm, Arthur Andersen sent an email to the firm's lead partner at the Houston office telling him to start destroying documents. That was like pulling the trigger on a gun pointed at Enron and Arthur Andersen unleashing the **corporate tsunami** that followed.

I will in this book talk **about the aftermath of** *"Enron"* and the corporate disaster of national scope It triggered. I realize that I use *"Enron"* in the corporate sense just as the world now refer to **"9/11"** in context of terrorism. These terms have become coined to mean far more than this single company and that single terrorist attack.

The victims of **10/11** included thousands of employees, probably hundreds of thousand who either lost jobs or careers but dramatically impacted their pensions altering forever their lives. Not just the people of Enron. There were many suppliers, customers and of course the shareholders whose investment were wiped out nearly in a flash. The employees of subsidiaries such as the electric company serving the Pacific Northwest and power plants worldwide Enron had acquired over the years became subjected to downsizing and bankruptcies.

Enron triggered a flood of corporate scandals over the remainder of 2001 and into 2002. Martha Stewart's infamous denial of a single alleged insider trade led her to be invited to a congressional hearing party joined by of course the Enron folk and **Bernie Ebbers** of Worldcom whose empire crumbled in mid 2002.

There, before the Congressional inquisitors, she along with the rest of the pack sang the same song "I didn't know" and no, I didn't do that and "no, I don't remember. **Martha's mistake** was to join the rest of that pack in those hearing and sing their song.

Had she admitted that single one time, one day sole stock trade to the SEC, she would have had to pay a fine of probably less than $50,000 and she could have gone back to her kitchen. She didn't cook any books nor take hundreds of millions the others took nor caused anyone in her company to lose jobs.

Martha was an easy mark for the Feds. The national urge was to find an easy one to convict and the feds nailed Martha, the queen of kitchen, who this time got to serve time in the federal pen for a few months.

**Bernie Ebbers of Worldcom** was another story. He and his Chief Financial officer Scott Sullivan did an easy thing to make the company look good to investors. Scott simply took $11 billion in corporate expenses and shuffled them over to the capital side thus creating earnings instead of losses and that's cooking the books. Sullivan admitted his guilt, cut a deal to testify against his former boss for a reduced sentence. Still, good ole Bernie kept singing the song "**I didn't know**" through his trial and was sentenced to 25 years in July 2005. The jury didn't understand how a CEO *could not know*. But Bernie has a good lawyer who convinced the judge of letting him out on bail pending the outcome of the appeal which could take months and even years. By that time, the current wave of public outcry against corporate fraud will have subsided and he might never take up residency in **Hotel Prison**.

The Rigas family which founded cable TV giant Adelphia was a different breed. They treated their public company as their private piggybank. Thanks to the Enron volcano erupting **10/11,** the lava flowing from its corporate fissure revealed that they simply stole $2.1 billion directly from their company and yes, their shareholders.

The Rigas family simply had the board (Father and Sons) authorize the use of corporate collateral to fund loans to themselves for their private use. Adelphia founder John Rigas, age 79 and his son were convicted in July of 2004 of conspiracy, bank fraud and securities fraud for looting the cable company and duping its investors.

Their action bankrupted Adelphia Cable, one of the country's largest cable TV operator with the assets sold to its competitors.

These people had one thing in common. They all were founders of their companies. As founders, they believed that their company was **'their company**" forgetting that they went to the public to raise billions of Dollars selling their stock to create those companies. Lest we forget, the true owners are the shareholders. They used their boards as puppets and did just about whatever they wanted. But, they forgot the fly in the ointment and in their case, that was the information explosion. The availability of detailed financial information and SEC reports via the Internet and modern communications to anyone with a computer and a wall jack plus $20 bucks per month access did them in. The irony is that Adelphia supplied that information via its broadband service while a division of Worldom provided one third of U.S. Internet backbone. They made possible their own demise. I bet you never heard this from anyone before, ever!

**No, I didn't forget Arthur Anderson,** the big, revered and respected accounting firm which was overseeing Enron's and Worldcom's books making sure none of this could ever happen. Arthur Andersen was the firm doing the auditing and advised these companies and others on strategic matters. This was the company assigned the job of keeping their client's books honest and accurate. Each year, they certified the balance sheets and all financials as accurate and put this statement in their client's annual reports. Andersen and other accounting firms received and continue to receive billions in fees for these services.

**How could this huge oversight have happened?** The answer lies in that old Russian proverb we often cite:

*"When money speaks,*
*truth keeps silent"*.

Going back ten years to *"Thieves"*, I devoted nearly the entire book to unraveling the **conflict of interest** mystery by presenting the financial services industry for what it was **and still continues to be**. How can a provider of a service go against the hand that pays you enormous fees? Would you go to the police and rat on your boss on whom you depend on for your livelihood?

Guess what? **I did just that**. I had an assignment from a public company and was ordered to issue a fraudulent press release and saw illegal activities taking place defrauding the shareholders. I refused, left the company and went straight to the appropriate law enforcement agency. Then, with my help, the CEO of that company eventually was charged with multiple federal indictments including securities fraud of which he was convicted. This didn't happen in 2001. It was well over ten years before.

Let's go back 20 years to the mid 80's when I was responsible for preparing the corporate forecasts for Eastern Airlines which then was one of America's largest airlines with revenues of over 4 billion Dollars. I was instructed to raise the forecast so that the company could meet the lending standards required by its banks. I refused to **"cook those books"** and got "retired early". Ironically, Eastern Airlines was liquidated in bankruptcy ten years before these type of scandals surfaced and its former leaders still bask in the sunshine unblemished except of course when it's time to "*meet their maker*".

Let's get back to Arthur Andersen which erupted as a national accounting scandal. Congress held hearings, the public cried out and the nation demanded something to be done. Congress heard and passed in 2002 a new law named the **Sarbanes Oxley Act.** This is such an important law that I will discuss it in the next chapter including examples of how it resulted in some unintended very negative consequences for corporate America.

I hope this legacy of Enron and presenting it as Corporate America's **10/11 disaster** offers you a better understanding of what's happening in the business of public corporations. Above all, I hope you by now realize that the corporate volcanic eruptions of 2001 were just that, adjustments to the *corporate plates* which over many years result in periodic quakes and tsunamis. They will over the years occur again because like the magna inside the earth is part of the earth's core, *greed is part of the human psyche.*

> *"Few men have the virtue*
> *to withstand the highest bidder"*
> George Washington

# Sarbox: The Great Accounting Reformation

The Enron/Worldcom accounting scandals enraged the nation and the Congress held hearings. The people demanded reforms to return trust and integrity so we again could rely on the blessings auditors bestow upon corporate financial statements. In its infinite wisdom, Congress in 2002 passed the Sarbanes Oxley law, now known as **SARBOX** for short.

The intent of SARBOX was good. CEO's were required to certify under penalty of perjury that their financial statements are true and accurate. This means that CEO's and CFO's (Chief Financial Officers) must not only know the financial condition of their companies, but they must also tell the truth or face stiff fines and jail. To make this possible and ensure no more Enron/Worldcom style accounting fraud, strict new accounting controls had to be implemented quickly with a year end, 2004 deadline. The new law also prohibited accounting firms from providing certain consulting services and imposed stricter corporate governance rules for the board and its directors. Sounds like a great deal doesn't it?

**Wrong!** Remember the days when we drove up to the gas station to fill up and pay for the gas when you knew how much you owed? Those days ended when a few gas thieves filled up and just drove off. Today, all of us are **treated like thieves** being forced to either pay in advance or swipe a credit card and get approval from the credit card company before the gas pump even turns on. The same thing happens in an office when someone gets careless or screws up. Instead of dealing with that person **strict new rules and procedures are created** and applied to all employees making sure that not a single one person could unintentionally commit a transgression.

SARBOX is no different. It assumes that everybody involved with accounting is a crook. SARBOX established a **"Public Company Accounting Oversight Board"** within the Securities and Exchange Act of 1934 thus adding a new oversight dimension to the SEC. This replaces an existing self regulation board within the accounting profession.

You may have already guessed where this is leading. A new bureaucracy imposing enormous new time consuming and added expenses to running public companies. Overnight, an entire new industry was created. **SARBOX Compliance.** Consulting companies specializing in this work came out of the woodwork like termites eating up corporate time and money. Computer programs were created to automate Sarbox compliance creating a boom business for the Information technology companies providing these services. Yes, the accounting firms are racking in billions in fees by devising detailed requirements for companies to be in full compliance with these new regulations. New spending required to meet Sarbox compliance for just one year, 2005, was estimated to reach **$6.1 billion**.

But wait. There are more regulations the government has placed on business leading to huge incremental costs. The HIPAA (Health Insurance Privacy Act), SEC and FDA compliance systems added another estimated $9.4 billion sending business a total $15.5 billion for just 2005. Who pays for this? **You and I pay for this**. This cost goes directly to reduce bottom line corporate profits or worse still, adds to losses. That, my friends, lead to lower stock prices. This is money sucked right out of a struggling economy and our individual pockets.

Ouch, that hurts in the worst possible way because this hits the general stock market at the very time it needed to get out of a slump. For example, one company with revenues of $95 million spent about $1 million in Sarbox compliance which reduced earnings by 3 Cents per share just for 2005.

Then shareholders got a double whammy. The company was forced to announce that it must **restate** one prior quarter for 2004 because it had a "**material weakness**" in internal controls. The company had issued new stock raising about $30 million and on the day it issued and announced that stock sale to one institutional investor, the stock went up on that good news. The Sarbox consultants six months later told the company it had to reduce its operating income by $10 million because that was the benefit the investor **received from the "market"**. Sarbox compliance required that the company had to go back and restate its financial results to include it as a "deemed dividend". While this didn't cost the company one penny nor makes any logical sense, **shareholders ended up paying for this lunacy.**

When the company issued the press release announcing this as a "material deficiency" in internal SARBOX controls, the stock tanked by 10% with shareholders holding the bag. The company of course had to pay for the press release telling this "good news" to the world and press releases can cost $1,000 with the wire services. The shareholders and the company continued to suffer for a time despite great news of new large contracts and revenue gains. Why? Because this "restatement" continues to show up in the company news every time an investor checks the company out.

**Here is another way the shareholders pay for this new burden placed on Corporate America.** Companies try to get their financial reports out to shareholders as soon as possible after the close of the prior quarter for all kinds of good reasons. Now, thanks to Sarbox, more and more companies delay their financial releases to coincide with the day the company also files its formal quarterly or annual report with the SEC. Why? Because Sarbox requires a meeting with the auditor each time it issues a financial report.

Since it takes typically about ten days for the company to file its formal full report with the SEC, a second meeting with the auditor is required because the company can't be relied on to properly disclose a potential material event which could occur even during the time between the press release and the SEC filing. To avoid this extra cost and personnel time, companies started early in 2005 to report their financials concurrent with the SEC filing thus delaying information to shareholders often to the SEC deadline which is 45 days after the close of the previous quarter.

**It gets worse** and yes, much worse. Some companies and especially the smaller publicly traded companies simply can't afford these new expenses associated with being public corporations. So they go private. That's great you might think because then, the company buys your shares and you get cash for your stock. Wrong! The company could also go Chapter 11 bankruptcy wiping the shareholders out with you getting **zero for your shares** and that has happened.

Thank Sarbox and the Congress for all this. But hey, the risk of corporate accounting fraud has been reduced. Yes, it has for the small percentage of the companies whose CEO's and CFO's steal and cook books. It's true that company books and operations may become more accurate. But at what cost?

**Yes, Sarbox is really great for the accountants, consultants and Information technology companies**. They took home an additional $6.1 billion in 2005 and that came right out of our pockets via lower stock prices because of lower earnings. Isn't that saying something for the guy in the White House who keeps telling us that we need **less government and more self management?**

## Life in the SARBOX
*Rely not on personal integrity and honesty, but on computers and systems.*

# Is Chapter 11 Bankruptcy
# A License to Steal?

Ever heard of the "*tip of the iceberg*"? That's what the Enrons, Worldcoms and Adelphia Cable were. Let's dig beneath these erupting volcanoes and see what other corporate mayhem goes on. There is a lot and I'll cover a few just to give you the flavor. Unfortunately, most of them happen without headlines, trials and jail time because no crime was committed. That is, no crime as defined by the criminal code or securities regulations. But yes, I call them "crimes" against shareholders, pensioners, employees and many others because a lot of money was lost and continues to be lost. Although they are not called crimes, they are the worst because the people committing them get away with them not only scot free, but with lots of money. Your money. The people who commit these "legal crimes" are very smart and often use their brains more to squeeze money from the corporate coffers than devising ways of running the business better. They often skirt the law and somehow, know just where not to cross the legal line although they cross the **moral and ethics line**.

To illustrate the degree of deceptive actions taken by supposedly respected people, I will now tell about real companies and actual situations, some of which still are happening as I write this book. There is no need to tell fiction here although I confess that these factual stories may **be juicier than fiction.** You be the judge if the CEO's and Boards of these companies belong in a hell where former shareholders are their slave masters and prison guards transported forward from the time of Genghis Khan.

I will describe real companies and what actually happened but I will give some of them fictitious names to protect my mortality since the companies and its principals still exist.

Once, there was a publicly held company named **Wireless** founded in the early 80's. The company went public in the early 80's and raised millions of Dollars over the next 20 years from shareholders to finance their existence and growth. That's as it is supposed to be for public companies. Founders raise capital from shareholders to operate and grow the companies. The shareholders become the owners of the companies with management running them and the board overseeing management. That's how the system is set up and supposed to be. But too often, as in this example, that's not the way it works out.

Back to **Wireless.** As happened with many companies after the 2000 election and 9/11, business slacked off and times weren't great. The cost of remaining a public company suddenly became a real burden thanks to Sarbox. The stock slumped from above $10 to below $1.00 and faced delisting which would make it difficult for the company to get more funding. But the company remained solvent, was current in the only bank loan it had and business prospects remained good. There was one dark cloud hovering since the company was formed. There were several family members in key top management positions and the board was filled with long term friends.

One morning when turning on the computer, the big bang came. Wireless **announced it filed Chapter 11 bankruptcy.** A buyer for the entire company was standing by to pay $4 million cash for the company including sufficient immediate cash to keep the company running. The company's attorney requested an emergency hearing in Bankruptcy Court to seek approval for the sale and the judge granted the request. So, two weeks later, the company was sold without any debt except for the mortgage on the Company's headquarters building which the buyer assumed.

The company owned its headquarter property which was appraised for $11 million with the mortgage of $7 million thus leaving a net asset value of $4 million. **Bingo!**. That was exactly the offer to buy the company and approved by the Court. Oh yes, there was the operating business built over a period of nearly 20 years with annual revenues of about $30 million which the buyer got for free. The estate received net $2 million after the court paid off the $2 million bank loan leaving about 25 Cents per Dollar to pay off the $8 million owed to creditors.

Here is the killer. **The buyer was none other than the CEO's brother-in-law!** The unsecured creditors screamed foul and the court appointed an examiner to look into the transaction. This led to a motion by the unsecured creditors to the Court requesting that it reverse the asset sale on the basis of impropriety. But, the Court ruled by denying that motion and this process took well over one year sucking up a significant amount of remaining cash bringing to the creditors 10 Cents on the Dollar if they are lucky. Making matters even worse, the CEO and the buyer filed a lawsuit against the attorney representing the unsecured creditors committee which they lost with damages awarded to the company officers. To settle this lawsuit, the creditors attorney agreed to terms including the reduction from 25 Cents on the Dollar to about 5 Cents which eventually will be paid to the creditors.

When this was all over, the former CEO still runs the company, his brother in law owns the entire company, the shareholders got wiped out and the creditors are still waiting for their 2 Cents on the Dollar over two years since the company filed Chapter 11. I had filed a claim for $15,000 for services rendered and will someday receive under the Court approved plan about $380 after waiting over two years.

The $2 million the buyer paid the "estate" to be distributed to the creditors was dwindled down to about $750,000 by the lawyers and the Court. In my view, this case reflects a criminal assault against the public sanctioned by the U.S. Bankruptcy Court. **But who will go against a judge of the Bankruptcy Court?**

No, this was not an isolated case. Let's look at **Starcom Corporation,** a solid little telecom products company founded about 40 years ago. Like **Wireless**, it fell onto tough times during the telecom meltdown. The CEO raised capital to operate the company by selling more stock to shareholders as the stock continued to drop, even into the pennies.

This practice is very bad because it dilutes the equity held by existing shareholders forcing them to either buy more stock to offset this dilution or sell at a huge loss. A much better way would have been for the Board to insist that the CEO find a buyer or merger partner for the company while it still had some value thus offering continued opportunity for shareholders. But no, the CEO is a stubborn engineer who insisted on hanging on, even if it was to a probable bitter end. He laid off half of the company and penny pinched saving the company nearly out of existence, despite strong objections to the board by a few shareholders. So, about six months before he filed Chapter 11 bankruptcy which wiped out shareholders, he raises another round of capital by offering a secured convertible bond. Guess who were the principal investors? The Board and a few close friends and even he, the CEO himself invests.

**Guess who inherited the company?** The secured bond holders of course, the CEO himself and his friends. Today, the company still exists and seems to be doing well. But only for the CEO, his board and a few friends. To his credit, this CEO did submit a plan to bankruptcy court offering stock to unsecured creditors thus at least doing the right thing by those owed money by the company, unlike the case of **Wireless.**

**Chapter 11 Bankruptcy** was created by Congress to give companies the chance to reorganize for a fresh start. Unfortunately, a rising number of companies are using bankruptcy laws to take public companies private by having the court erase shareholder equity.

Under the Bankruptcy Reform just passed in the spring of 2005, bankruptcy is made much more difficult for the individuals who also are shareholders in public companies. Unfortunately, nothing was done to prevent company boards and CEO's from abusing bankruptcy laws to steal the companies from shareholders. This is yet another example on how **government participates in defrauding shareholders and taxpayers.**

## *"When Money speaks, truth keeps silent"*

# Corporate Obituary
# and
# Coroners Report

It's mid summer, 2005. Yet another remnant of an old line company was placed into the **corporate graveyard** after holding a funeral in bankruptcy chapel. It really is like a funeral because when a company's assets are sold via bankruptcy, it ceases to exist. When the judge's gavel comes down the day he approves the asset sale representing the company's business, the **pallbearers** lower the casket into the ground. Oops! Almost forgot to mention that the **pallbearers are the lawyers**. Once the asset sale is completed, the "estate" receives the money the buyer paid for it and "**corporate probate**" begins. This is the process whereby the court decides how the estate assets will be distributed to the inheritors who typically are creditors owed money by the former now dead company. The final act is the reading and approval of the "Disclosure Statement" in court presented by the attorneys for the "estate". This is like '**reading the will**" after a person has died and all parties have agreed to the disposition of all remaining assets in the estate. After that day, the company becomes a memory to some and a nightmare to former employees and shareholders who lost their jobs and the value of their shares.

**Proxim ,** a Silicon Valley high tech company entered its **coma state** on June 13, 2005 when its lawyers filed Chapter 11 in Bankruptcy Court  declaring a financial emergency. The emergency was that the near comatose company must sell its functioning body parts quickly to an able buyer who was willing to graft them onto his business.

The lawyers representing the comatose corporate body named Proxim urged the Judge to immediate harvest the still barely alive body parts and place them into another body or they too would die.

**Proxim** was the company originating as Western Multiplex which had for 30 years developed microwave communications networks. Then, in 2002 the company acquired Proxim and took its name. The latest acquisition was the Orinocco product line from Avaya which still is the remnant of Lucent Technology which was created when the original AT & T was broken up by the U.S. Justice Department. When I discovered Western Multiplex, it had good potential to participate in the coming high speed wireless networking revolution, plenty of cash and revenues of about $100 million annually.

The acquisitions of Proxim and the Orinocco product line added about another $100 million in revenues. The company raised over $150 million in new capital to finance these acquisitions and provide additional operating capital. Instead of integrating and properly managing these business units into a single efficient company which had the most extensive product offerings in the high speed wireless " space", **revenues declined.** By the summer of 2005, the company ran out of cash and warned of a probable bankruptcy. The stock had tumbled from about $250 to 30 Cents as of the time Chapter 11 was filed even after it did a ten for one reverse split late in 2004 which raised the stock from 90 Cents to $6.00 in January 2005. The investors who provided nearly $150 million over the past several years refused to once again bail out the company.

The final death for shareholders came mid June , 2005 when Proxim's shares were delisted from the NASDAQ, traded down into the pennies and fell to the Pink Sheets where it likely will trade as a shell. The shareholders had lost it all.

**What was the problem?** How could this company fail in the face of the first stage of an industry which is set to boom for years having missed the Wi-Fi stage and just entering the beginning of Wimax which could last for years worldwide?

The problem was **management** and the failure of the board to effectively **oversee** this management and replace it in time. Later chapters in this book will address the board of directors problem as it is a structural deficiency in how public corporations are overseen.

The day Proxim filed Chapter 11, June 13, I sent the following letter to two board members, the CEO and chief financial officer. As you read it, I want you to realize that such a letter could be sent to many companies which failed thus ruining investment portfolios, employee pensions and the lives of employees and shareholders.

**Gunther Karger's letter to Proxim's CEO and Board the day Chapter 11 bankruptcy was filed June 13, 2005**

Six **months ago**, when it became apparent that the company was suffering a cancer condition called **GAD**(Greed, Arrogance & Disrespect) I recommended emergency **surgery** followed by **chemotherapy** in the form of draconian restructuring and the cleansing of its corporate culture. The prescription called for selling off non core assets or closing them down to create fresh capital for the remaining smaller company. The chemotherapy was the bringing in a new CEO purging the corporate body of the bad cells. Instead, you voted yourself repriced options, hired an outside firm to sell the business and gave yourself personally bonuses for effecting change in control or selling the company.

**That reflected disrespect** for the owners who are the shareholders, the investors and the employees who toiled hard for years building good products and solid marketing channels.

You especially failed to honor the heritage of Western Multiplex, Proxim and Orinocco which created for you extraordinary opportunities. There is no doubt that, despite problems integrating merged business elements, the market opportunity and the capital you were given several times should have resulted in Proxim today participating in the emergence of an exciting and fast growing business.

Today, you commit what is in reality **corporate homicide**. It's homicide because as you file Chapter 11 via an expedited asset sale, Proxim **ceases to exist** as a "person" which is the entity of corporation is in the eyes of the law. As happens when a "person" dies, the assets go to the estate which distributes them via probate court in accordance prescribed legal procedures. It is **Aggravated involuntary manslaughter** because although you did not intentionally kill a "person", the shareholders who were the legal owners received a dead carcass having the value of only a tax loss. The funeral is the ceremony called the **Confirmation of the Disclosure Statement** presided over by the bankruptcy judge. It is **aggravated** because you caused it via the application of incompetence and ignored wise counsel. Unfortunately, instead of a jury convicting you of **Aggravated Manslaughter** causing you to face prison time, a Bankruptcy Judge will render a **directed verdict** of **not guilty** while the victims weep in disgust as moral justice will not be served.

You could call me the **Corporate Coroner** who examined the body and determined its cause of death. I close the case stamped

*Proxim: Cause of death was "GAD"*
*Greed, Arrogance and Disrespect.*

# Corporate Meltdown
# In Montana

This may be one of the worst corporate disasters seen in recent years. Chances are good you haven't even heard about it because no one was indicted, no trial was held and I doubt there even was any investigation. It's an example of corporate greed at its worst and total disregard for employees, shareholders and ethics. I must include this case because it illustrates what so often happens as a result of present weakness in board of directors oversight of companies. Without any doubt, there is critical need for a change in corporate oversight by the board of directors. Be sure to read the chapter in this book where I present serious and substantial reforms in the present system.

**The Montana Power Company(MPC)** was founded in 1906 as an electric utility company to provide electric power to Montana. It was created with money from Montana citizens and eventually became one of the most profitable utilities in the country paying a 7% dividend to its shareholders. The stock traded on the NYSE in the $40-60 range benefiting from Montana's utility regulation which set a rate structure guaranteeing a 13% return for the company. With over about $3 billion in assets and 3500 employees who had steady jobs with solid pensions, MPC was a good corporate citizen of Montana.

Then the craze of deregulation hit the power industry in the late 1990's. The Montana legislature passed its deregulation bill in 1997 giving electric utilities the freedom to sell generating assets and go into other forms of businesses. This created the opportunity for MPC to **"*maximize" shareholder*** "values and it hired the New York based investment banking firm, Goldman Sachs to tell management how to do it.

The advice Goldman Sachs gave MPC was to sell utility assets for more than $3 billion and move MPC into the exploding Internet based telecommunications business where fortunes were being made and stocks soared. MPC's management bought that plan and with the approval of its Board sold all utility assets generating about $3 billion in cash. Management then renamed Montana Power to Touch America and spent most of that money laying 18,000 miles of fiber optic cables which was to support the coming boom in new Internet traffic. Goldman Sachs was paid an estimated 20 million in fees for providing **investment banking services** plus much more for acting as the "broker" in the selling of the assets. Now get this. Four top MPC executives were paid more than $5 million in bonuses for making all this possible. The MPC executives including some on the board received bonuses totaling millions.

**But what happened to the utility business and the employees**? The company which bought most of the electric utility business went bankrupt, the Internet explosion had already happened and since the 18,000 miles of cable laid became excessive capacity, **Touch America went bankrupt**. But you should know that before Touch America filed for bankruptcy, the Board paid key Air Touch America managers $500,000 additional bonuses for helping the company execute its bankruptcy plan.

Eventually, all employees lost their jobs and their pension was severely reduced and a great, profitable 100 year old company was essentially gone. The stock crashed from $60 to 30 Cents and was delisted by the NYSE to the Pink Sheets. One employee who retired from Montana Power after working there 27 years losing $350,000 in his 401K retirement reflected what happened to many employees who thought they worked for a solid utility company which couldn't possibly have serious problems. After all, everyone needs electricity and gas in any economy, boom or recession.

Shortly after all this was over with 3000 employees losing jobs, pensions and more, **the CEO moves into his new $3 million house built from bonuses** received from Montana Power. How could all this have happened? Where was the board oversight in all this? Who did the board really represent? Who benefited from this and who lost? The answer lies in the following: **Conflict of interest.** If we "*follow the money trail*", we see the answer. The board and executive management stood to benefit personally and dramatically by doing all these things. Instead of executing their fiduciary responsibilities to the company, employees, its shareholders and customers, these **birds** smelled gold and placed it into their own nests.

Wait a minute**! Isn't this stealing**, self dealing, conflict of interest and committing fraud? **Yes,** it is based on **moral and ethical standards.** But in this case, no **criminal law** was broken and therefore, there was no prosecutable crime. The Executives proposed the actions, the Board approved them and there were the legally required disclosures made to regulatory bodies such as the SEC.

Unfortunately, the Montana Power case, as bad as it was, is just one of many we hear about. Except of course the employees, shareholders and their families who suffer. That's why we need to meaningfully reform the system of corporate governance which is the fancy name given board oversight of publicly owned companies.

*"There is no fire like passion, there is no shark like hatred, there is no snare like folly and there is no torrent like greed"*

Buddha

# The Silicon Valley Raiders

No, this is not about a sports team. It's about a corporate raid destroying not only a fine old line company, but also robbing its shareholders. Unfortunately as in the Montana Power Case we just addressed, no one was indicted nor will anyone ever go to jail. This is about two persons who in simple form stole over $200 million and left the company in ruins while they sailed into the California sunset not to be heard from again. They vanished with the shareholders money. Yours and mine.

California Microwave was one of the world's pioneering companies making microwave communications systems serving industry and government. Revenues from the Government division alone exceeded $100 million annually. During the "heydays" of the telecom explosion, the Board of Directors decided to "freshen up" the company and brought in a new CEO and his friend who became the CFO. Together, this duo, a "his and her" team had a plan to transform California Microwave into an exciting new company focused on the wireless high speed Internet which then was in the development stage.

By the year 2000, this new team had sold its consistently profitable government division and a few other operations, acquired a development stage British company and renamed itself to Adaptive Broadband. The focus shifted to the priority in making sure the investment world would know about the wonderful prospects about Adaptive Broadband. A full time investor relations staff was appointed with a Vice President in charge who did an outstanding job. Investors and institutions snapped up the shares which rose from $10 to a high of $210 in one year. We did so well that this one stock paid for a great cruise and we bought a new Chrysler convertible Limited for cash.

Along the way, huge contracts for the new products were announced with prospects for revenue and profit growth for years to come. One such company awarded a huge $500 million multi year contract to build future generation broadband equipment. When I noticed that this particular company was a penny stock company trading on the Bulletin Board and didn't have adequate financial resources to finance such a large contract I became concerned. This concern heightened when the company lent over $10 million to another small company to finance its purchase of the new equipment. It usually is not a good idea to sell product to anyone who can't afford to buy it and depends on you lending the money if you also are the seller. That's "buying the business" which causes us to revisit Barry Minkow and ZZZ Best in the mid 80's we discussed in an earlier chapter.

I really got nervous when I noticed SEC filings showing that the CEO and his lady friend started to sell large number of shares which they had acquired with options grants. I called the company about this but was assured that this was a "personal asset diversification" program. We had started to purchase stock in this company while it still was California Microwave at about $10. However, when it went over $100 and we saw the insider selling along with the other questionable practices, we started to "trade" the stock all the way up to $200. This limited our risk as we no longer were long term investors. When the stock had fallen to about $50, we bought back thinking that it had corrected to reasonable buying level. But when the insider selling continued along with more questionable corporate practices, we sold out at about $30.

A few months later when the stock was down to about $15 another California Company made an offer to purchase it for $17 per share. Then the next shoe fell on the company and its shareholders. One morning I saw the terse announcement that the company was restating its revenues and announced huge losses along with the CEO and his CFO resigning.

The company which had offered to buy Adaptive Broadband pulled out of the deal and the stock crashed. The company filed Chapter 11 bankruptcy, the stock tanked into the pennies. Class action law suits followed and the company was liquidated. Today, there is nothing left.

But wait! The CEO and his CFO friend (who incidentally was a lady) had long since **flown into the California golden sunset with well over $200 million**. What about the employees and their pensions? Evaporated into the sunset as a vapor trail created by the burning worthless stock certificates.

Whoa there!!! **Who allowed this corporate mayhem?** Where was the Board of Directors who were responsible for oversight of this company and its executives? That's a good question and I have dedicated a chapter just on this. **What about the SEC?** That government agency received all the filings promptly by the required deadlines. All the insider stock transactions were duly filed and no, we then didn't have an Eliot Spitzer, the New York attorney General who has been doing what the regulators failed to do.

### *"When money speaks, truth keeps silent"*
A Russian proverb


Let's now add a Persian proverb

### *"An egg thief becomes a camel thief"*

# Can Forecasts Manipulate The Truth?

Forecasting is a "tool" driving major decisions for industry and government policy. The basic purpose for business is to ensure that " **just the right" resources will be available as future revenues roll in and for government to make the right policy decisions.** Forecasts can project economic downturn or growth leading to adjustment in resources to match the projected results. The **heart** of forecasts are the **assumptions** on which the projections are made. **Making the wrong assumptions or worse yet, making the forecast based on self serving interests can be disastrous.** Forecasting a minor storm when a hurricane is  coming leads to major disaster. Making business forecasts based on hope or self serving interest can lead to the demise of corporations and enormous financial loss to investors.

**Here are a few examples of forecasts which were dramatically missed** leading to demise of companies and irreversible damage to industries and serious damage to our national economy. Prior to 1980, the airline industry was experiencing double digit growth and the airlines ordered airplanes and planned terminal facilities based on forecasts which projected a near perpetual continuation of this growth. The forecasts were also based on the reality that a majority of people had never flown **but ignored** the fundamental assumption that growth could not be continued at that rate when this relationship reversed. In came airline deregulation in 1980 coupled with economic slowdown in the early 80's. The forecasts were missed on the downside by a wide margin.

**A second reason** the forecasts were missed was that the projections were not sufficiently adjusted downward in "rate of growth" based on the dramatically increased traffic volume. **That was a statistical error** made by the young managers coming out of graduate schools who based their forecasts on their own limited experience and statistical models lacking the experience of reality.

**Faulty assumptions** was the principal reason why the projections were missed on the downside by wide margins. It turns out that "forecasting" was my responsibility at Eastern Airlines for 15 years when it was a $4 billion corporation. I learned a great deal about how it should be done but more importantly, how **it should not be done**. I was the person who in the early 80's told the President of that airline **not to buy one billion Dollars of aircraft and he laughed in my face**. I was right and he was wrong but he was in charge and the airline eventually failed. (make sure you read the chapter on why Eastern Airlines failed). His decision **using wrong assumptions** contributed to that company's eventual demise ten years later. This industry is today an economic disaster resulting from excessive aircraft capacity bought to serve a demand level that did not exist. That process added billions to the airlines long term debt aggravated by the unexpected impact of the cost of terrorism and dramatic increased cost of fuel. American Airlines is the only major U.S. airline which had not filed for bankruptcy by the fall of 2005 when Delta and Northwest landed in bankruptcy court.

**A similar problem occurred in the late 90's** during the Internet's initial dramatic growth and all that came along with it. The telecom industry invested heavily to meet the projected demand created by the Internet industry's growth based on straight lining the forecast and ignoring basic business principles. **This led to the telecom industry meltdown** followed by derivative meltdowns of related and even indirectly related industries and the demise or restructuring of many companies. Forecast error played a key role in creating this economic disaster.

One result of this process is the demise legendary AT&T which in the fall of 2005 was acquired by SBC. Thus, the company started by Alexander Graham Bell, the pioneer of telephone communications ceased to exist as an independent company. Let's go back further in history. Do you remember **Western Union,** the pioneer of telegraphic communications? Western Union was the first company to install a transcontinental microwave network providing "trunk" capacity similar to what fiber optic cables provide today. It turns out that I was the person who helped engineer this first transcontinental broadband wireless network so this is from personal knowledge. The leaders of Western Union **assumed that** their systems would not become technologically obsolete for a long , long time and therefore failed to invest in new technologies. **That company failed.** We haven't heard of Western Union for many years. Today, it is a wire money transfer facilitator bearing no relationship to the original company except in name.

The Iraq war was based on the **assumption** of a "quick in and out" technologically driven "**Shock and Awe**" operation to last just a few months. The assumptions also failed to take into **account** the structure of the Iraqi people, their long term heritage and the absence of significant internal existing military forces that existed in Afghanistan which were instrumental in defeating the Taliban. The Iraq war was based on the **assumption** that weapons of mass destruction and the capability to deliver them existed in Iraq. We now know that was a false assumption, faulty intelligence and based principally on political strategy to support the political interests of George Bush and his backers. **That led to the disaster it has become.**

My point in this is that leaders can assume anything they **wish** to support their agendas and then issue their forecasts to support those **assumptions**. That can lead to disaster as evidenced by the above major examples.

Forecasts must be based on solid information, intelligence, technological, demographic and economic trends. Basing forecasts on political or corporate agendas by individuals or special interest groups nearly always leads to business disaster. **Forecasts must be done by professionals** who know how to do such things and be allowed to do this relatively independently. The forecast is really an appraisal and should never be done by the same people responsible for achieving such forecasts. If they do, it would be similar to a homeowner doing his own appraisal he takes to the bank for the loan and that becomes self serving and the banks won't allow that. If the leaders want to still pursue their agendas, they of course can but they then must also assume responsibility for such decisions and share the consequences.

**Corporate executives who ignore these principles** will likely eventually see their companies suffer leading to shareholder loss. **Heads of governments who create self serving forecasts** and ignore these principles which are as solid and fundamental as is the Newton's law of gravity can lead their countries into economic disaster. The Bush administration is an example witnessing the gross missing of the Medicare Prescription Bill projections which rose from the $400 Billion presented to Congress at the time of its passage to a near double $750 billion. Another extreme example of the catastrophic consequences of making self serving forecasts is the New Orleans **Hurricane Katrina disaster.** When the Corps of Engineers proposed a budget item in 2001 to repair and improve the levees protecting New Orleans from flood in a predictable strong hurricane, the ████████ent rejected that funding on the assumption ██ would hold and that New Orleans would not ████ a serious storm until the funding crisis created by the Iraq war had been resolved. That was a tragically wrong assumption which led to the destruction of New Orleans in a $200 billion disaster, the worst our country ever had.

Although we witness the demise of corporations when their forecasts are badly missed on the downside, worse still, some executives will cross the line to **"cook the books" by adjusting financials to "meet the forecasts".** Enron and Worldcom are well known examples of this problem with their executives going to jail for doing it. The motivation by business leaders is to generate higher compensation via bonuses and the exercise of options. Government leaders **manipulate** the forecasts via self serving assumptions to get elected and secure greater power.

The U.S. government deficit disaster and the Iraq War is still going on for nearly three years as of the time this book was written. This was projected to be a quick in and out exercise and is another example of acting on forecasts based on faulty assumptions.

**What's the answer to minimize this problem?** In both industry and government, forecasts should be done by professionals, not the very people who are responsible for achieving them because that nearly always results in serious conflict of interest issues eventually leading to disaster. Corporate executives as well as heads of state must maintain an "open" policy allowing people of independent thinking to examine the assumptions and prepare forecasts to ensure that they are reasonable and based on broad considerations.

*"He who lives upon hope,*
*will die fasting"*
Benjamin Franklin

*"Wishful thinking i͟ ͟*
*disastrous  unwished results "*
Gunther Karger

# Truth or Consequences
# Spin the Numbers

Truth or consequences was a comedy show hosted by Art Linkletter who is one of the greatest of all TV personalities. Just think of the material he would have to work with the past few years. The California energy crisis, Enron and Worldcom balance sheets, Martha being stewed in the kitchen and all the corporate mayhem we by now know about. Art would have a field day while we would have had a wet laugh after wiping out the tears thinking about all the money lost and the great companies destroyed.

Have we learned the lesson that there is a consequence of not telling the truth about corporate financial statements? I doubt it. While the recent revelations and their consequences may still weigh heavily on our minds and especially, our wallets, I am very sure **cooking the books will return** in a bigger and hotter corporate kitchen in a few years as investors and regulators become once again complacent. We just don't know yet in what form and when.

Cooking the books and accounting fraud is what we have heard about and continue to learn more about daily as new situations jump up from under the rug. Let's now talk about another form of corporate mayhem involving the financial statements which I call *spinning the numbers.*

The news release announcing the quarter's financial results quote the Chief Financial Officer "We were gratified nearly meeting our goals given the circumstances". However, the numbers reflected a 30% drop in revenues and an increased loss compared to the prior year. But, he continues *"the bottom line was better than we had expected"*.

The spin here is that the bad news is presented as good news. The reality that revenues declined and the loss was greater was downplayed. Not said is that if this trend continues, the losses will decline as revenue also falls until finally, **it all ends in the book called Chapter 11.**

Let's spin the top again and we come up with **GAAP vs non GAAP earnings.** GAAP stands for "Generally accepted accounting principles" as defined by a national accounting board. The "GAAP" earnings reflect the bottom line including the net of all pluses and minuses. Non GAAP exclude writedowns, restructuring costs, asset sales and other non recurring financial statement items and typically reflect pure operating results inclusive of debt service expenses. Normally, non GAAP results are better than GAAP and yes, you guessed right, that's why companies so often focus on **non GAAP** and even disclose both routinely. Non GAAP can also be called **pro forma** when a company has been involved in a merger, asset sale or is in process of discontinuing some of its operations. All this gives lots of opportunity for **spinning** the financial results to look the best and often better than they really are. Just like politics. Shine the light on what makes the politician look good and put the rest into a dark corner where you might not look. The same often applies to financial results.

**What does all this mean?** You should spend more time on the small print and footnotes in the company's financial report rather than focusing on the company's news release. Look at the trend of reported results and how the company performs against its own expectations. Too many restructurings and fund raisings to make up for revenue shortfalls are red flags. A favorite trick is to blame a revenue shortfall on the temporary delay of a large shipment to one customer. *"Although it could not be booked in this quarter, it looks promising for the next quarter"*.

What's the best you can do about company releases and financial results? Spin the top yourself and let it rest on the SEC filings instead of the company's press release. While the SEC filing may often seem bleak and full of "howevers", it tends to give the worst case scenario causing you to look a little more, think about it more carefully and find out what areas of the company's business you should be concerned about.

*"Get your facts first, and then you can distort them as much as you please."*
Mark Twain

*"If you get all the facts, your judgment can be right;*
*If you don't get all the facts, it can't be right"*
Bernard Baruch

# Accounting Scandal Touches
# The *Saint* of Wall Street

**Spinning the numbers on financial statements** is so important that I will devote an entire chapter to just one case illustrating the magnitude of this problem. Guess what? This problem is still with us two years after the enactment of government accounting reforms. The old Russian proverb 'When **Money speaks, truth keeps silent"** to which I often refer to in my book 'Thieves on Wall Street" and lectures on corporate fraud again "speaks loudly" for what's happening on Wall Street".

Early in 2005 , Eliot Spitzer, the New York State Attorney General revealed that there were accounting problems at insurance giant AIG(American Insurance Group). The allegation was that the financial statements issued by that titan of American insurance industry may not have been as forthright as they should be. AIG's venerable 79 year old chairman, Hank Greenberg was called to task for this problem.

This was about the transfer of $500 million in premium income from AIG to Buffet's Berkshire Hathaway while retaining this $500 million as revenue in AIG's earnings statement to make AIG's financial statement look better not only to prop up AIG stock, but to enhance insurance reserves. In principle, this is not much different than the **"book entry " manipulation** that happened in Enron and Worldcom.

Just days after this new 'Wall Street investigation" surfaced, other transactions began to unravel such as a $2 million transaction reversal between a unit of Berkshire Hathaway and an Australian insurance company.

Incidentally, there is a practice between insurance companies called "**reinsurance**" which distributes risk over many insurance companies. This is a good practice because it reduced concentration of potential loss to one company in the event of major disasters. What unfolded early in 2005 was taking this practice to the "**greed level**" and that's when trouble comes to investors and eventually, the creators of these advanced forms of getting extra money from shareholders.

The actions at AIG were taken to make the financial statements look better than they really were. I call this "**balance sheet cosmetics**" which hide the "wrinkles" and make the books look better than they are. It is the "high tech" way of "**cooking the books**" making it difficult for the investors to know what's going on and encouraging them to invest more and sell less thus propping up the stocks.

The Berkshire matter is in principle worse than the others because it involves the "**Rabbi of the Street**", Warren Buffett whose judgment thus far has been known as impeccable and is considered the "**oracle" to whom all flock for advice.** Although it's highly doubtful that he was personally involved and had agreed to help unravel the mess, confidence in his "**oracleship**" could ratchet down a notch.

Shortly after this scandal surfaced on Wall Street, Hank Greenberg who built AIG and headed it for 40 years was sacked by his board from all his positions. The executive who headed the Berkshire Re-Insurance unit involved with these questionable transactions resigned and the cleansing process had begun. On May 25, 2005, The NY Attorney General filed a civil suit against Greenberg charging him with ordering his trader to buy AIG shares to prop up the stock price. This is an alleged securities manipulation to benefit personal shares as Greenberg owned millions of shares of the stock. As of the time I finished this book late September, 2005, indictments of high General Reinsurance officers were expected.

Once again, it took a courageous individual in the right place to address problems the SEC and other regulators should have dealt with long ago. Investors should induct Eliot Spitzer into the *"Investors hall of fame"*.

*"Dare to struggle and dare to win"*
Chairman Mao Tse Tung
Founder of the Peoples Republic of China

# Class Action Lawsuits
# The Lawyer's Gold Train

The concept of "**lawyer or attorney** " is to represent a client's best interest in matters involving the law. The concept of "**Advocate**" represents a broader responsibility often assumed by a lawyer as he ensures that the interest of his client is always best served. The keyword here is *best interest.*

The most frequent controversy occurring in client representation is conflict of interest whereby the attorney or anyone representing someone's interest benefits in some way from the **winning by the other side.** For example, if you are the mayor of your city responsible for the best interest of your citizens and take a bribe from a developer for giving favorable treatment, you are in a situation of **conflict of interest.** You benefit personally and financially at the expense of your people who elected you and pay you for your services. Bribing public officials is a crime punishable by jail sentences and big fines.

Real estate agents are another good example illustrating the principle of conflict of interest. The agent represents either the seller or the buyer but never both except in limited cases where both parties mutually and in writing agree to use the agent as the facilitator of a transaction. All parties must have a clear understanding from the very start of a potential transaction as to who represents whose interest. Real estate practices and law is very specific about this and for good reason.

The seller has to know that he will get the best price for his property with the best possible terms and that his agent will do his professional best to make sure that happens. How can the seller, who is the agent's client, know that happens if the agent also benefits in any way from the buyer's side?

Now that we have gone through great pains to define conflict of interest, let's get back to business. Corporate business involving shareholders and that's you and me. Let's refer to the chapter "**Is Bankruptcy a license to steal?**" There, I give the details of how the management of a publicly owned company with $30 million in revenues and $4 million in net real estate assets was sold to the CEO's brother-in-law for a net of $2 million to the "estate" belonging to creditors and shareholders. By the time the lawyers dragged this case through the court for over two years, there was only about $300,000 left over for the creditors and zero for the shareholders. Just one law firm collected $300,000 with others about $245,000 and they got 100 Cents on the Dollar for what they billed with the rest of the creditors getting **3 Cents on the Dollar**. I personally had filed a $15,000 claim for money owed and as of the time this book is completed, I am still waiting to receive my paltry estimated $400 after waiting for nearly three years. The law firm which got the $300,000 helped the company structure the bankruptcy and had the company agree to a "**secured debt**" forcing the Court to approve the priority payment nearly right after the filing for 100 Cents on the Dollar.

A recent patent infringement suit between two companies taking about two years of court hearings sucked about $2 million in legal fees from the small company defending itself. The company eventually went bankrupt after losing the case. But the lawyers got their $2 million right up front.

**Now, let's go to the class action attorneys**. This is an industry spawned by the rise of the high tech industry in the early 80's. Here is how it works. The company develops new products and discusses their prospects with investors who buy stock in the company. Unfortunately and too often, the expectations go beyond what the company actually generates in revenues and earnings.

Revenue shortfall could be due to internal company problems, external industry trend changes and frequently, it's the economy not behaving as the economists predicted. Sometimes it's just plain bad management.

A shareholder files a lawsuit against the company charging it misled the investors. The law firm representing the investor advertises nationally for other investors in the same company offering to represent them in a lawsuit to recover damages resulting from losses in the stock. A bunch of them sign up and we have a "**class action**" law suit against the company filed by the law firm on behalf of the shareholders. Typically, the law suit is filed by a named "lead plaintiff" on behalf of all investors who bought and sold that stock within a specified time frame called the "class period".

The law firm will typically seek damages from the company in the millions of Dollars based principally on how much money the company has in its balance sheet and the level of liability insurance it carries. If the company has little cash, is about to go bankrupt and no insurance for this type of claim, the law firm likely will not file a lawsuit nor proceed, even if the lawsuit is well justified. There is no one to pay huge fees. The rule is "no deep pockets, no class action law suit". The cases are taken on by the law firms as a *contingency case* meaning that it will take on the case without any significant retainer fees nor charges for litigation expenses. However, the firm gets a big chunk of the eventual settlements plus recovery of all expenses right up front.

Most of the cases are settled before they go to trial because the companies either can't afford the expense of defense in a drawn out trial or just want for it to go away because it depresses the stock preventing the raising of new capital in stock offerings. Rarely is any significant money left over for the shareholders on whose behalf the cases were settled with most going to the law firms.

The big California law firm, Millberg Weiss became the largest law form specializing in class action suits and defined the industry it became. Over the past 30 years, this one firm has filed and processed hundreds of class-action cases **and won tens of billions of dollars in settlements and judgments against companies.** A few years ago, the firm split into two and even the Congress passed a bill limiting the rapidly growing class action *lawsuit industry*.

As so often happens, **greed and power** sets in when money rolls in too easily. It seems that the pot is bottomless until the **monkey wrench is thrown into the Dollar making machine.** That happened late June of 2005 when the Justice Department charged a client of a large New York class action law firm with fraud, conspiracy, money laundering and obstruction of justice. The indictment alleges that the law firm paid millions of dollars in **secret and illegal kickbacks** to the client and members of his family to become a plaintiff in over 50 class action cases from 1981 to 2004. During this period, the law firm paid this client and his family more than $2.4 million while the law firm collected at least $44 million in legal fees where this client and his family were plaintiffs and clients of the firm. As of the writing of this book, this matter is proceeding with indictments and likely criminal charges.

I would be remiss not mentioning an **insider trading** case involving class action lawyers. The Wall Street Journal reported on September 27, 2005, that a California judge balked at a settlement between the CEO of the giant software company Oracle and class action lawyers wherein he would donate $100 million over five years to charities if he pleaded no contest to the alleged charges. What was he accused of? Selling $900 million of his Oracle stock within 30 days of the company issuing a warning of lower than expected financial results. The SEC law prohibits any insider from trading stock of its own company within a specified quite period prior to a public release.

**The question I ask is**: "How can the CEO of a company not know about his own company's financial status within 30 days of a release about it?" **The Judge asked** "Why should the lawyers get $22.5 million for handling the case with the company shareholders paying that horrendous bill? Here is the clincher.

The $100 million proposed gift over 5 years would really not be much considering he typically gave about $100 million per year anyway and all of that would be tax deductible. What shareholder restitution would this be considering that the cost of the shares likely were very little since they probably were very low cost founders or optioned shares? I include this late breaking news just before "going to bed" with the book because this illustrates how shareholders pay while lawyers get rich and the alleged perpetrators get off nearly scot free.

**Now, let's see where all this money comes from**. We know where it went. The money comes from the corporate treasury and the insurance companies which receive hefty premiums from the client companies. Guess what? The corporate treasury money belongs to the company and the company belongs to you and I, its shareholders.

It's our $44 million which went to the above referenced law firm and its single plaintiff clients and that's just a very small part of the billions which are involved in class action suits. That money should have remained in the treasury to generate interest income and pay for corporate growth which is the reason investors buy stock.

When a company pays out money for these things, earnings decline leading to lower stock prices. **Worse still,** often the lawsuit settlements include the issue of new stock to the law firm as added compensation. That dilutes the common shareholder's interest even more by lowering the company's earnings per share as there will be more shares outstanding.

This money belongs to the company and the company belongs to its shareholders and that's you and me. It's up to us to make sure the company's management, its board and the agencies regulating the lawyers know how we feel about this. Fortunately, today we have email, fax and conference calls through which we can communicate our concerns.

*"If we desire respect for the law,*
*we must first make the law respectable"*
Louis B. Brandeis, Supreme Court Justice

# What's the Latest Insurance Scam?

## *Credit score premium adjustment*

**Insurance:** *Guarantee against the risk of loss to be paid by a third party such as an insurance company. The risks such as fire, storm, theft, liability and the amount to which these risks are insured are stated in the insurance policy.*

**First, a little primer on insurance.** Many states force you to have car insurance to get your drivers license. It's either to get the insurance or park your car. Want to buy a home? The banks force you to buy property insurance. They won't let you close on the house until you have bought the level of insurance they tell you. If you read the fine print, you'll find that the banks will buy insurance for you if you let the policy lapse and put the premium on the loan balance. You can bet that will be the most expensive insurance your money can buy! If your house loan is greater than 80% of the price of the house, the banks force you to buy PMI which stands for private mortgage insurance. This insures the banks against you not paying your mortgage. The banks aren't satisfied getting your house, evicting you and then selling it. You pay the premium but the bank is the beneficiary.

**There is more.** When you buy a house, the "system" forces you to buy title insurance guaranteeing that the title to your property is "good" and there is no lien on it. You pay a lawyer specializing in title examination to go all the way back to the time when the white man took the property away from the Indians or when the first settler laid claim to government land. Title analysis must be performed each time the property is sold and you are forced to pay the premium to a title insurance company which issues to you a title policy.

You either buy this insurance or "they" won't let you close on the house. That's not all. You have to update this insurance if you refinance your mortgage or take out an equity loan using your house as collateral.

These are but a few examples of the "system" **forcing you to buy insurance** for various reasons if you want to drive or buy a house. I exclude medical or life insurance into this "forced" insurance category. You could go without medical insurance because you can't afford the premium but you risk going broke, losing your house and car and go bankrupt should you ever have a medical problem. It's estimated that about 40 million Americans don't have medical insurance because they simply can't afford it. They go to the county charity hospital and take their chances. You also could go without life insurance and many people do. But then, if you die while your kids are young, you could leave your wife in a financial disaster trying to support herself and your kids without the income from your breadwinning job.

Insurance is a perfect cash cow for the legitimate industries such as banking, real estate and financial services. They can set premiums at almost any level they want. Sometimes like car and home owners property insurance, they have to file their rates with State Insurance Commissioners but more often than not, they get the rate hikes they seek and you pay like it or not.

**Here is the way it works**. You are the cow being milked and the insurance company is the milking machine. They send their agents out to attach their tentacles to your wallets and simply turn on the switch watching the money being sucked out. When they want more "milk" than you are willing to "give", they simply increase the "suction" and there always seems to be more money if you want the insurance, which the system requires you to have. You simply find a way to pay even if it means getting it from other "parts of your body", keeping in mind still that you are the cash cow.

What's the latest in insurance "*scams*"? I put the word scams in quotes because I am taking editorial license to use it broadly. Typically, a scam is an illegal way to squeeze money using some type of scheme. You may note in this book that we cover mostly schemes which **aren't illegal** and some even blessed by the government. Whether a mugger assaults you on the street robbing you of your wallets and your valuables or a slick investment scheme causes you to loose your money, the effect is the same. **You have lost your money.** The mugger may be caught and put into jail but the slick investment salesman laughs all the way to the bank while you at a later day are too embarrassed to tell anyone about it.

**Let's get right to the latest scheme. Raising your insurance premiums reflecting your credit**. Wait a minute!. Insurance is supposed to be based on risks against which you have no control over. What's your credit to do with insurance premiums on your car or your house? You guessed right, nothing. You have driven your car for 20 years without a single accident or ticket but you get seriously sick or get laid off your job and miss a credit card payment one time for more than 30 days. When you get the next year's car insurance bill, you notice that the premium went up significantly and you call your insurance agent. You get the bad news. Your credit score dropped.

Guess what? Your credit score can drop for any number of reasons having nothing to do with your driving habits or even creditworthiness. **When you apply for credit**, like a home mortgage, switch cellular phone provider, rent a new apartment, get a new credit card, open up a new brokerage account or, in recent years, apply for a new job, **"they" pull your credit report** from a credit bureau such as Equifax, Trans Union or Experian. The credit bureau records this as an **adverse event** and that can reduce your **Credit Score** by as much as 20 points if you have more than one credit inquiry within a six month period.

Let's say you are shopping for a new mortgage or car, and within a few months, there were several such inquiries to the credit bureau. Your score could drop as much as 50 points. The range of credit score is from about 400 reflecting high risk to 830 at the lowest risk. Let's say that you are at 725 which reflects **low risk** which is considered good. But because your credit report was accessed for any or several of the above legitimate reasons, your score drops to 675 to **medium risk**. That easily could trigger an increased premium for your car insurance as more and more auto insurers have over the past several years started this practice. You complain because that has nothing to do with your driving habits. But your insurance agent will tell you that the high risk drivers often also have low or no credit. While that can be true, they have just put you in the same category as the temp day laborer working from hand to mouth and who drives a broken down 20 year old car. You complain bitterly but you pay because the law requires you to have auto insurance which leaves you no choice.

The very latest in insurance is to use a credit score in determining your home insurance premiums. This is being proposed in Florida as this book is written. The same principles apply as in auto insurance. Here is the case where you may live in a great upscale neighborhood with houses selling for half million Dollars.

But because of the way the system of using credit scoring works, you may be compared with a person living in a blighted urban area subject to high crime.

**Here is a new way for the insurance companies to squeeze more money from your pocket** and which is also being proposed in Florida by the major insurance companies. You have one non storm claim and your premium goes up as much as 20%. What that can mean is that you may be a person without any non storm claim in 30 years and suddenly, a water pipe breaks, you have water damage and you file a claim.

You might have paid $15,000 in premiums over that 30 year period without a single claim and now, for a $1000 claim, your premium rises 20%. That sounds ridiculous but that's what the major insurance companies have requested the Florida Insurance Commissioner to approve .You guessed right, it probably will be approved and creep into most states.

**What's the right and fair way to set insurance premiums?** The premiums should be based on risk factors applicable to that individual and the category that individual may be in plus where he lives as environment can impact risk. **But it should be true risk**. Using factors such as credit scores without putting some logic applicable to that person is simply a new way to legally squeeze more golden "milk" from the cash cow and unfortunately, we all are on the same farm being milked. But unlike the cows who can only "**moo**" when milked to excess, we can e-mail and go public with our concerns thus handing a lot of **embarrassment to the insurance companies** and the State Officials responsible for insurance regulations. We can also vote for someone else at the next election. Of course, we could find a hungry lawyer and file a lawsuit against the insurance companies citing unfair practices and the regulators for failing to do their job.

# Boiler Rooms Go High Tech

I went to work in a boiler room before I wrote "**Thieves on Wall Street**" ten years ago so I could give you the real flavor of what that was all about. The rows of small cubicles with a broker, a rolodex and one hand held telephone are gone. Today, we have computer generated calls milking the cash cows, people like us, in a variety of ways. We have brokers sitting in front of computer screens, creative investment artists creating professionally looking websites and emails looking like messages from long lost friends written just for you.

**The penny stock schemes** still come down, but today it's on email more than on your phone. But, the telephone still does ring. Back then, they hawked companies with no or nil revenues and zillions of shares outstanding. They tell you how to make a quick $10,000 by buying 100,000 shares at 5 Cents per share and sell it in a few weeks for 15 Cents when that expected great news release comes out about the new gold mine discovery. Today, the boiler rooms have a new product. Worthless shares of bankrupt companies whose cancelled shares trade in the sub penny range in the pink sheets. All assets have long been sold in bankruptcy court and the shares represent nothing more than shell corporations with no assets, no operations, no employees and no office. But the name of the company still shows up over the stock symbol and you can get an instant quote on your computer screen.

Just think, you could have made 100% or doubled your money if you had bought Astrocom shares for 0.03 Cents and sold it for 0.06 Cents. You could buy 1 million shares for just $300. Here is your chance to buy a million shares, a once in a lifetime opportunity.

Sure, you do your due diligence by looking up the company which happens to be Astrocom Corporation with a great looking website. The company makes a leading edge product making it possible for businesses to have 100% reliability Internet connection, a legitimate product. The company has an office, telephone and is real. You buy the million shares feeling real good. But then you may later check further to learn that Astrocom is now a privately held company where a few investors and creditors own it with new nonpublic stock.

**The stock you bought represents no business, no products, no employees and no revenue.** You bought an empty shell of a former publicly traded company which went private via bankruptcy court. You sell your million shares and feel lucky to get 2 Cents per share having lost $1000. **Who made the money?** Aha. Just like I wrote ten years ago, the market makers made it on the spreads and the brokers on the commission. I suggest you get my first book, *Thieves on Wall* Street which remains as valid today as then when I devoted chapters to the details of this business. The Pink Sheets are full of these kinds of situations and ripe for the pickings of boiler room operators who bring them to you in gold trimmed websites and your e-mail.

Do you remember the letter you might have received years ago from a **very official sounding Nigerian gentleman offering you a million Dollars** for the use of your bank account to deposit an inheritance or large commission from a business deal? It's still coming but now directly to your computer vial e-mail as well as very officially looking quality air mail.

Today's business has become global as I discuss throughout this book. Although I focus principally on fraudulent schemes in the United States as we have plenty of them without me going overseas, the emails and calls you get can come from anywhere.

Modern technology now facilitates offshore boiler rooms anywhere in the world out of easy reach of U.S. regulators and law enforcement. When the phone rings or email beeps, it could come from Boca Raton, once the investment fraud capital of the United States or Islamabad, Pakistan under the protection of Osama bin Laden.

*Just like I said ten years ago when the penny stock broker calls...simply hang up.*

*Today, I add the word "delete" when you get e-mails from people you don't know offering to make you money.*

# How Hedge Funds
# Clip Your Wallet

**Hedging**: The process of protecting yourself financially by initiating a counter balancing action; to evade the risk of commitment

We hear about hedge funds and how the smart folk make a bundle. When was the last time you made money with a hedge fund? Do you know what a hedge fund really is? You better know or you could risk losing your "shirt" and may have to trim real hedges for your next meal.

The hedge funds were created to help institutional investors protect their investments from unexpected turns in the market into the opposite direction. It's like insurance. Hedge funds have become very popular because until very recently, they were exempt from the federal regulations covering stocks and mutual funds. Hedge funds can offer investors classified as "Accredited Investors" products such as private placement exempted from most regulations although they must start registering with the SEC based on new rules being implemented as this book goes to press.

The principle is that an "accredited Investor" is supposed to know more about the risks and be able to afford losing his investment more than the average investor. To qualify for this elite class of investors, you must have at least one million Dollars in assets or demonstrate that you make at least $250,000 per year income. It's estimated that in 2005, hedge fund investments exceeded the Trillion Dollar mark. Most hedge funds are responsibly managed but the investor needs to pay close attention to avoid being sucked into potential money losing schemes.

Who can start a hedge fund? Anyone. Hedge funds can be started in a bedroom, on a boat or the kitchen table by anyone ranging from a solid investment banker with offices on the top floor of your tallest financial high rise center to a con artist with a mail box and living out of the trunk of his car. What do you need to get started? All you needed, until now, is the gall of creating a great sounding investment plan and the sales ability to convince large investors to part with their money to make a killing. You offer the investor a high return on their investment and you take out a high percentage of it for your profit. The Ponzi Scheme in some way was a "hedge fund".

I came close to getting involved with a scheme which would have provided huge returns for the investors. My telephone rings and it's a man named Ackhabar from Houston TX. He wants me to participate in a currency exchange program where he offers to sell Kuwait Dinars(currency) at a discount to market price. He claims to represent the King of Saudi Arabia where he worked in his "Court". I called "Nizzar" who I know is a relative of the King being the nephew of His Highness principal financial adviser living in Switzerland. Nizzar confirmed to me that Ackhabar did actually work for the king as his chief procurer of western women but had fallen out of His Highness grace due to poor "merchandise". I didn't call Mr. Ackhabar back.

I came close another time to getting into one of these juicy deals when I maintained an office in the same building as a group of business brokers. They asked me to participate in a sure fire currency deal where huge amounts of money could be made through a "bond discount roll" program. All I had to do was to bring in a few substantial investors who would put a small deposit in a fiduciary account and the money would start rolling in.

The two partners in the business brokerage business were so sure of this deal that they put deposits on a Rolls Royce and a Bentley. We all came to the "office" at 3 AM to get ready for the "tranche" to start in Zurich, Switzerland.

We all anxiously awaited for one person to call the principal banking officer with a critical banking code to activate the transaction. We kept on waiting. Finally, after the close of business Zurich time, a call came from someone in Chicago who also was part of the "network". He gave us the sad news. The person with the critical banking codes had failed to make that last crucial call to the Zurich bank by the deadline and the deal was dead. They all had frantically been tracking down that critical "fiduciary" who last was seen making a telephone call from a bar in Scotland. The deal having died forced the two business brokers to cancel their Rolls Royce order and instead went around the building taking up a collection to help pay the phone bill.

This true story played out in the early 90's. Today, September 12, 2005, there is a lead story in the Wall Street Journal about Bayou Management, a hedge fund managed by the 46 year old son of a New Orleans respected financier. This story surfaced about a month before when suddenly, the fund's manager closed the business into which prominent investors had invested over $400 million and none was returned. The telephone had been disconnected and the federal authorities launched an investigation. The Sept 12 story in the Wall Street Journal reported that $100 million had been discovered being transferred from one bank to another all around the world in a scheme supposed to make huge profits into the billions. As of late September, 2005, indictments are imminent but it may be a problem finding and arresting the "investment banker" who seemed to have fled the country for some safe financial haven abroad.

We come down to the same old thing. What's changed since Ponzi, Tino di Angelis, Enron and all the rest? The schemes get bigger, more complex and high tech and fancy names. Beyond that, they are the same. Just as there are some good and honest hedge funds and honorable business brokers, there are rotten eggs in the basket and it pays to open your noses and smell the sulfur.

# Here Comes Government Deception

The Medicare prescription bill Congress passed is an insult to seniors while Medicare Fraud continues unabated as a cancer ready for chemo. The government tells us our economy is robust strong while oil soars to $60 per barrel sucking one third of the GDP growth out of the economy. We are told we must send our troops to a country full of terrorists and weapons of mass destruction and find none after spending $200 billion of our money and we lose close to 2000 soldiers with the civilian population of Iraq suffering over 100,000 casualties. Then, both sides destroy the country's infrastructure and we are told we make progress. We visit the murky domain of oil and see how oil billionaires make more billions while you pay nearly twice for your gas at the pump. Then, we learn that we should have faith in all this in the name of God with people questioning whose God we are to believe? It appears that we need a renaissance in Washington to restore reasonable balance between the ultra liberals and the conservative radicals. It's time for a little truth from those we elected to serve us, the people.

As we go to press with this book, another and maybe the largest deceptions in American history surfaces in Hurricane Katrina which devastates the upper Golf coast and drowns New Orleans. With all the focus on Homeland Security and quick reaction to disasters which could be terrorist or natural, people thought they were safe as all the billions of Dollars surely would have implemented systems and plans for dealing with such. How wrong they were. The incompetence at all levels, local, state and especially federal was staggering. Be sure to read the chapter on this sad day in American history.

# Washington's Insult to Seniors
# The Medicare Drug Act

Horror stories are routinely reported about senior citizens having to choose between food and prescription drugs. We heard about seniors having to order drugs from Canada where they could get the same drugs much cheaper while Washington regulators did their best to convince them those drugs were unsafe. Pills costing $1 each were considered cheap as seniors struggled with medicines costing them $200 per month plus for just one medication.

My wife, Shirley was on Tamoxifen, a post breast cancer medicine costing in 2002 about $100 per month which caused us to significantly exceed our monthly maximum limit imposed by our health insurance company. We were able to buy three months supply of this exact same medicine from a pharmacy in Carson City, Nevada which scoured the world for best price and quality for just $45. This compared with the $300 it would have cost from our local drug store using the system created by our government. **I call that not only a disaster, but a government mandated fraud intended to benefit the drug companies at our expense**.

The American public became enraged at this abuse of our wallets while the drug companies profits were soaring. Politicians demanded relief and especially for the seniors who at their stage of life need more medicines while getting less income in retirement. Candidates for political office, especially the presidential office, used this national crisis to gain votes promising relief. **So what did Washington do once it's new president was elected?** Congress passed a bill providing seniors a prescription benefit through Medicare.

We all **sang hallelujah** and danced with tamburines praising God. We now could get our medicines, feel better and live longer without first going broke. But as the details of this "manna from the heavens" unraveled, we realized that it was mostly a tale right out of the fairy book. Most of the seniors got less than they had and the **rejoicing was replaced by more cries of another foul played on the Washington ball field.** Let's go to the details of this great plan Washington served on the Senior platter.

First, although the Congress passed the bill in 2003, it would not go into full effect until 2006 and that's beyond the life of some needing relief immediately to extend their life. On an interim basis, the law encouraged private companies to issue "drug discount cards". This triggered a flood of such cards, typically offered for up front fees. But they were complex, interfered with many plans seniors were already on and became quickly ineffective. Some states offered local discount plans based on income and asset means tests with thresholds so low that to qualify a person must be impoverished and probably already unable to get any medications except what their doctors give as samples.

An important provision in this new law was that it became **illegal for Medicare to negotiate prices with the drug companies thus guaranteeing price fixing and accelerating costs for seniors.**

This provision is totally contrary to the American free enterprise system of letting the market and best deal makers rule the price of commodities sold. This provision allows the drug makers to use the "cost plus" method of pricing their drugs. They just add any cost to the price.

Let's look at just one example of cost abuse. A typical ad on prime time TV would be for a drug beneficial to cancer patients in chemotherapy experiencing dangerous low blood counts resulting in severe weakness sometimes even leading to blood transfusions and hospitalization.

**We know about this because that happened to Shirley(my wife) in 1999 when she underwent surgery, chemo and radiation for breast cancer**. She was in such bad shape that I had to carry her to the car to get her to the hospital for blood transfusions and she didn't eat for days. Only then, the insurance company authorized this type of blood count improving shots costing $500 per shot and that's daily for ten days after each chemo treatment.

This is the type of medicine the drug makers advertise on prime TV spending millions. Why would anyone ever want to take this medicine knowing the condition required to need it? Is this something to promote on prime time TV selling to the general public? **No!** Every time this ad came on the screen, even now, years later, Shirley tells me to turn the TV to "Mute" as she remembers how she was when she needed to take that type of drug. Advertising Dollars spent on this type of non elective medication is simply thrown out money and yes, your money because the drug makers just add the cost of these and other similar ads to the cost of your pills. Our government, yours and mine made it illegal to negotiate drug prices for senior citizens by a provision in the Medicare Drug Benefit Act of 2003. I call that "legal fraud" because in any reasonable business context, it is legalized price fixing and price fixing is typically an illegal act punishable by stiff fines and jail time. **But that's what our government did in 2003** by including the price fixing provision in the Medicare Drug Act.

**Another provision** of this much heralded great drug benefit was the initiation of a monthly $35 premium to be deducted from Social Security checks. For us, that means another $70 per month expense translating to $840 per year. That could be a significant 5% reduction of annual Social Security income for many seniors who can ill afford that extra expense. But, by paying this premium, you become eligible for a 50% discount on your medicines after paying a deductible of $250 per person.

That's a discount off the rapidly increasing drug prices made even higher as a result of Medicare's inability to negotiate drug prices and you can't be covered by any other insurance having a drug benefit. If you are on this plan, starting January 1 of 2006, the **benefit stops** when each covered person has spent $2,250 and that's per year again, kicking in when you have spent a total of $5,100 and that's per person. If there are two of you, you must spend annually $10,200 before that plan again kicks in. If the two of you received $30,000 annually from Social Security, this means that you must spend 30% of your entire Social Security income just to get through this "doughnut hole" of Medicare drug benefit.

In its wisdom, the Congress provided some relief for low income senior citizens by waiving the monthly premiums and offering drugs for a low $5 payment. **That's great if you pass the low income and asset means test**. Your total income must be less than $14,355 for individuals and $19,245 for **married** couples. Excluding your home and your car, your total assets must be below $11,500 for individuals and $23,000 for married couples. According to a study by a leading research firm, about 60 percent have life savings of about $51,500 for singles and $63,000 for married disqualifying about two thirds of all 43 million Medicare recipients.

**What's the bottom line?** The cost of this great program is estimated to be about $535 billion over a ten year period and that goes directly to your income tax bill. The majority of all seniors will totally miss out on this program and for most, it can increase their drug expenses.

That's what Washington gave the American Senior Citizens. Our government claimed it is a great new benefit as it alleviates the rising misery of declining health care and sky rocketing medical costs. I call this "**Government Fraud**" because that's what it is.

120

Politicians telling the American public it will get a benefit if elected and then delivering this program is a " bait and switch" technique often used in car show rooms and less than honest business deal making. It's the same old story. "***When money speaks, truth keeps silent***". This time it's the government and the drug industry speaking. It's time the American public started to speak up strongly to send the message of "**Truth or Consequences**" to the White House and the Congress.

Isn't this a gross insult to the senior citizens of our country? We are the ones who fought in WW I, WWII, Korean War, Vietnam and built our country's industry to where it is. **Don't we deserve more respect?**

*"You can fool some of the people all the time and all the people some of the time, but you cannot fool all of the people all of the time"*
Abraham Lincoln

# Medicare Fraud
# A Cancer Ready for Chemo

The form I received from Medicare in the spring of 2005 informed me that a medical equipment supplier had submitted a claim on my behalf for a motorized invalid mattress rental for the prior six month period asking Medicare to pay $3,462. I was shocked because I am thank God not an invalid, have never needed such a device nor had I ever heard of that medical supply company.

I immediately filed a report with the FBI Medicare Fraud Division and notified our local police department which initiated an identify fraud case since my Social Security Number had been criminally used. This also forced me to file a report with the Federal Trade Commission and credit bureaus to flag my credit file for potential credit card fraud since my identity data had been compromised. I tracked down the medical supply company at a Miami address and called to request them to stop billing Medicare on my behalf and possibly learn more about this. I could not find a single person at this company willing to speak with me in English. The detective coming to our house tried calling in Spanish but only received an answer service responding with an English message.

A few weeks later, the news was all over the local media about a North Carolina Medicare billing company involved in a scam defrauding Medicare out of several hundred million Dollars with many arrests. This was the same billing company sending me the notice about my six month invalid mattress bill. Shortly after these arrests, I received another notice from Medicare that the same medical supply company had submitted another bill for even more money.

It's widely known for years that clinics, doctors, medical supply companies and yes, hospitals are involved in Medicare fraud schemes such as my invalid bed. Hospitals submit bills for unnecessary services and supplies, doctors bill for unnecessary services including even operations, pharmacies for undelivered prescriptions and yes, bills are even submitted for services not rendered and on occasion, for identities created using dead people with new false Social Security numbers. A high concentration of this problem has been observed in South Florida perpetrated mostly by foreign medical people and even doctors practicing without a license. We are not talking about millions. This is about billions, it has gone on for years and continues to go on and on with no end in sight.

Meanwhile, insurance companies squeeze seniors by reducing benefits, increasing premiums and making it tougher for people to get medical assistance. HMO's are dropping good hospitals and specialist doctors from their networks forcing many seniors into clinics with marginal medical personnel. Shirley (my wife) had a bone scan scheduled but was referred to another medical diagnostic center where we had to request a translator because the technician spoke no English and we couldn't communicate. Yes, this was in Miami, U.S. not a banana republic further to the south.

While these and worse scams and frauds continue across the country, our representatives in Washington cry about Medicare being financially unsound and about to go broke unless it's fixed. Thus far, the principal fixing they have done is to allow Medicare to raise the Part B premiums for Seniors which just about wipes out the cost of living raise given them by Social Security.

**I call this defrauding our Senior Citizens and the tax payers.** The Congress and the White House should be held responsible for this disaster, much of which could be avoided if they addressed and **resolved** our country's real issues.

# Oil: Is There a Conspiracy?

**Conspiracy:** to join in a secret agreement to do an unlawful or wrongful act; an act which becomes unlawful as a result of the secret agreement, to act in harmony toward a common and unlawful end; The process of committing fraud.

**I would bet there is**. But read on and decide for yourself. I write this book as the price of oil hit $70 per barrel and gasoline crossed $3 per gallon for Regular with the motorists shaking their heads for answers while their wallets empty out at the gas stations.

The Arab oil minister blames the shortage of U.S. refineries for the high gas price. The economists blame declining supplies in the face of a global exploding demand for oil. The politicians blame prior administrations for a lack in foresight in not promoting more aggressively alternative energy sources and the environmentalists for preventing the exploration of the Arctic oil reserves. Hurricane Katrina legitimately raised the price of gasoline about 25 Cents per gallon as some refineries and pipelines were damaged. This led to a decrease in oil consumption which should have decreased the price of crude oil. Instead, it rose from **$65 to $70 per barrel which is clearly unjustified**.

Foreign policy experts blame China for growing too fast thus draining the oil reserves too rapidly. The commodity traders blame a severe winter using up too much heating oil and now, that the summer is near, we face an energy crunch from a hot summer which needs record energy to cool us down. A book could be written about why oil prices are high but I will tell you why in just this chapter.

Searching for the answer leads us once again to that old Russian proverb *"When money speaks, truth keeps silent"*. We will "**follow the money trail**" for surely at its end we'll discover the real truth about all this. Can I prove what I am about to say?

No. But as is done in the courtroom and you are my court, I will present clear facts which will lead you, the juror, to what will be reality and probable truth. I will present a scenario which looks like a giant worldwide conspiracy so horrendous and vile that you might not want to believe it. If you think I have gone into the dark reaches of a spy novel replete with international intrigue and terror supported by the highest and richest levels of world leadership, **you are not wrong.** If you think I am writing fiction, just focus on the plain verifiable facts I present herein and decide for yourself whether this **Is fact or fiction.** When in doubt, just ask yourself this question: *"Who does it benefit?"* **Follow the money trail.**

Let's get right into our search for the truth about oil.
Oil was just under $10 per barrel in 1999, just six years ago. The oil industry was in a slump, exploration was down with drilling rigs piling up on shore storage dumps. Many oil wells were shut down and capped because they couldn't produce profitable oil. But the U.S. economy was doing well, unemployment way down and our treasury was even showing a surplus with the national debt being paid down and politicians looking for ways to reduce taxes. Clearly, the oil industry leaders were scratching their heads for ways to stimulate revenues.

The first easy step was for **OPEC** (Organization of Petroleum Exporting Countries) to cutback oil production. We need to mention right now that OPEC consists of eleven nations all except one being predominantly Muslim. The exception is Venezuela which today is led by a very anti American dictator. The lead nation in OPEC is Saudi Arabia which produces about 30% of OPEC's oil. OPEC is headed by the Saudi oil minister who is a member of the Saudi royal family.

History has shown that international conflict, particularly military actions in the Mid East can have dramatic and quick impact on the price of oil. The following oil prices are given adjusted to the Dollar as of the year 2000 to give an accurate comparison. The Yom Kippur War in 1973 saw doubling from about $10 to $20 resulting from the oil embargo and closing of the Suez Canal to make oil shipping difficult. That's when we remember the long gas lines here.

The next trigger was the Iranian revolution in 1979 seeing oil spike up to about $40 then reaching nearly $60 in 1981 when the Iraq–Iranian war started. But oil dropped down to about $10 by 1985 to again spike up to about $25 during the short Gulf War in 1991. The price didn't hold and again dropped to $10 by 1999. Through a series of production cuts, OPEC managed again to bring oil to about $30 by early 2001 then to again see it drop to $20 by summer 2001 despite a giant 5 million per barrel daily production cut. Clearly, a more dramatic event was needed to stimulate higher oil revenues to support the spending and investment appetite OPEC nations and its leaders had become accustomed to. The Arab nations were building their cities into super modern metropolises and financially supporting their citizens with money derived from oil revenues. This appetite is based on more than love of money. It is based on religion.

The Koran (Muslim Bible) teaches Islamic expansion and world dominance. The Mid East conflict between Israel and its neighbors since its founding in 1948 and the rising world terrorism is testament to this philosophy. The Saudis and most Arab nations provide huge financial support over the years to terrorist groups such as Hamas and Islamic Jihad. It is estimated that Iran alone annually provides the Hamas and Hezbollah more than $100 million to support their terrorist operations.The Islamic insurgents, with the help of the U.S. managed to throw the Russians out of Afghanistan and installed the Taliban.

**Osama bin Laden**, a member of one of the most prominent and richest Saudi families led the ouster of the Russians and he become an honored guest of the new Taliban regime in Afghanistan. There, he planned and carried out the 9/11 terrorist attack on the United States that triggered the next increase in oil prices as the war on terrorism unfolded. Where did his money come from? While his family in Saudi Arabia disavowed any support for Osama's terrorist activities, his money had to come from somewhere and that somewhere principally could come from no other source than his family fortune. Although it can be said that the bin Laden family's fortune was derived from its construction business, the money to pay for all that construction and their investments came from **oil revenues**.

This time, not only did the Muslim oil nations benefit from the eventual rise of oil to $70, they profited from the dramatic decline in the Dollar against the Euro, a dramatic rise in Islamic world power and the opportunity to see a weakening of America in world politics.

Let's paddle further up the river of money toward its source. We'll head toward Saudi Arabia to estimate what the War of Terror brought to its treasury and that of the Kingdom's friends. Oil prices rose about $30 per barrel since just after 9/11. Multiplying OPEC's daily production of 29 million barrels by the average $30 per barrel rise results in the **daily revenue increase** to OPEC of $870 million.

This becomes about **317 billion new money in just one year** and this has gone on for several years since 9/11. This huge sum is more than half of U.S. federal deficit projected for 2005. The Saudi production of about 9 million barrels daily alone generated about $80 billion incremental money per year to the Royal family and their oil producers. The oil producers earned nearly $400 billion just from oil exports in 2004 and world consumers paid $1.2 trillion more for oil in the current year vs the prior year. This is more money received for selling the same oil at nearly zero incremental expense and is **pure profit**.

We cannot ignore the possibility that there is a grand scheme driving the **flow of gold** so we continue to head up the **river of money to seek the truth**.

This huge cash horde being amassed by the oil producers and receivers of oil royalties becomes what is known as **Petro Dollars** meaning excess money made from petroleum. Where does this money go except to enrich the already rich Arab treasuries? Much comes right back to the United States as investments in distressed properties, business and cheap stock created by a lousy stock market. A weak Dollar would greatly benefit the Petro Dollar investors if they use Euros instead of U.S. Dollars for these investments. But that's bad for U.S. investors going overseas with their investment Dollars. It also drives up interest rates in the U.S. eventually giving the foreign investors a higher return for the cheap Dollar denominated investments.

**What else would be good for the Petro Dollar investors?** Rising inflation and federal deficits in the U.S. That would increase interest rates giving a higher return on bond investments and result in making an eventual killing in rising real estate values all bought at about a 30% discount because of the declining Dollar vs the Euro.

As we approach the headwater of the river of gold, we start to sense some logic. Terrorist attacks instilling fear cause oil to rise and new money to be created via oil price increases to fund the rising tide of Islam. A war against Iraq and elimination of Hussein who is considered a rogue would strengthen the Saudi regime and its oil sheiks with the bonus of giving the Saudi controlled OPEC control over more oil and pricing.

**Elimination of Saddam Hussein** coupled with the liberation of that country's oppressed Shiites could lead to an eventual alliance with Iran and its Shiite fundamentalist Islamic rulers adding even greater world power to the world of Islam.

128

Then, we see a glimpse of the "western skies" as we get closer to the golden oracle upstream. The oil service companies with their idle rigs need to use them to drill for more oil. The high oil prices create political pressures to explore the pristine Arctic for new oil fields and open up the Florida Gulf coast for off shore exploration. Their eyes really start gleaming at the prospects of refurbishing old oil wells, constructing new refineries and pipelines around the world.

A "shock and Awe' war** destroying much of Iraq would create a huge multi year multi-billion Dollar opportunity to rebuild what was destroyed and modernize Iraq's oil industry. A war also would create a rise in fundamentalism within America which could lead to political unrest resulting in a **shift to the "right" and eventual reduction in freedom for the people.** This, coupled with a declining American economy would be a plus for the Arab dominated oil industry and could increase their control of America's business while harvesting the gold this strategy produces.

**Along the way upstream the river of gold we come to China** which is blamed for a major part of the oil price increase. We were told that the dramatic growth in China placed huge demands on its oil consumption. Let's get real about this. China's oil consumption in 2004 was just under 5 million barrels per day.

This compares with the U.S. daily consumption of 20 million. A 20% increase in China's oil consumption and that's a huge percentage leads to only 1 million barrels per day increase. This added demand is easily met by just one country, Saudi Arabia, increasing its daily production from 8 million to 9 million barrels. Saudi Arabia announced late April, 2005 that it could increase daily production immediately to about 11 million barrels and would spend $50 billion for new exploration resulting in a daily capacity of 13.5 million barrels.

In this context, we should also realize that the Russian oil exports are rising as their petroleum production becomes modernized and the many oil rigs around the world start pumping. How can it be credible for anyone to say that the oil prices have doubled in one year just to meet China's increased demand?

**Oops! I almost forgot to stop in Chicago** down town at the Mercantile Exchange Building. That's where the oil prices are set by commodity traders yelling at each other setting oil futures contract prices. **Did you think the oil ministers set the oil prices? If you did, you thought wrong.** The oil ministers and OPEC do **control the oil supply** and cause these traders to raise their future expectation of the impact of those production limits set by these ministers. The traders also react to major events such as oil rigs and refineries blown up by terrorists, earthquakes and storms damaging pipelines rigs. While these traders set the prices, the ministers control the factors driving price changes. Therefore, they have **opportunity to manipulate oil prices** to suit their self serving private interests.

**And now, we finally have arrived** at the head of the river of gold. There is a board of directors meeting in progress under a tent. We see the Saudi oil minister and other OPEC leaders from Iran, Indonesia, Venezuela. But we also see leaders from the West including oil tycoons from Texas and political leaders from Washington.

We see heads of private firms such as the Carlyle Group which receives billions of Dollars from its partners to buy America's businesses. Some of its partners are the oil sheiks as well as well known Houston oil barons. These are the nations and people **who so vastly benefit from world terrorism, rising oil prices,** inflation and rising interest rates. They are counting their money which came from our pockets, yours and mine. They smile as they hear the report that the gas stations collect twice as much for the same gas sold the prior year.

They are the people who bought our businesses on the bargain table and in bankruptcy court. Here, we also discover who helped our country become a little less free and more dependent on them collecting trillions of oil Dollars from world economies. They give a toast in celebration when they hear the report on how much greater power they have gained over the world.

**Is this scenario for real or is it a piece of fiction written by a paranoid cooking up a global conspiracy? That's for you to consider and history to reveal.** My responsibility here is to present a probable scenario based on facts so we can gain a better understanding of what could be happening. Hopefully, this perspective and understanding can help us guide our leaders toward different directions and policies.

**I must mention the Tea Pot Dome Scandal** during President Warren Harding's regime in 1921. Rumors floated around Washington that Secretary of Interior Albert Fall was spending large sums of money. On April, 1922, the Wall Street Journal reported that Fall had leased **Teapot Dome,** a strategic national oil reserve to Harry Sinclair, his friend. The Senate initiated an investigation into the oil reserves and Albert Fall. President Harding suddenly died on August 2, 1923 and was succeeded by vice-president **Calvin Coolidge.** An investigation revealed that Fall had received bribes of about $400,000 to award leases to petroleum companies owned by Fall's friends one of whom was Harry Sinclair.

On 17th October, 1927, Harry Sinclair was put on trial and charged with conspiracy to defraud the United States. The trial ended prematurely two weeks later when the government presented evidence that Sinclair had hired a detective agency to shadow the jury. Sinclair was tried for criminal contempt of court, found guilty and was sentenced to six months in prison. Secretary Fall was forced to resign.

*"Follow the money for it leads to the truth"*
Gunther Karger

# The American Tsunami

In 2001, the Corps of Engineers which is the federal agency responsible for flood control, submitted a proposal to upgrade the New Orleans levees which had aged and no longer may be effective in a major Category 3 plus storm. The New Orleans levee system is a critical dam system protecting much of the city against the waters of Lake Pontchartrain and the Mississippi River. Without this protective system, New Orleans would today be a lake because it sits below sea level. This levee system is critical even during sustained heavy rains because the city pumps the excess waters out of drainage canals into the River and the lake.

Failure of this levee and pump system during severe storms could place the entire city of 500,000 under water. This could render the city uninhabitable by creating a bio hazard nightmare as the electric system would fail causing the sewage mixing with flood water exposing the people to killer bacteria typically seen in third world countries. Such an unthinkable event could trigger a killer epidemic of contagious diseases as refugees flee the city causing casualties beyond the city.

**Scientists had been warning for years** about global warming and its potential impact on the earth's eco system. A particular concern is the warming of oceans which could lead to killer storms because hurricanes and cyclones feed on warm water. The warmer the water, the stronger the storms become. The Gulf of Mexico is especially subject to this warming because it already is naturally warm and somewhat protected against the cooler Atlantic currents.

The global scientific community under the auspices of the United Nations met in Kyoto, Japan in 1997 and established the "Kyoto Protocol" which set standards for industrial emissions and smoke stack controls to limit global warming for future years. This protocol was subject to ratification by participating nations. When George Bush was elected in 2000, one of his first acts was to oppose this environmental protection program on the basis that it would be excessively costly to industry and the scientific community had not yet proven the adverse potential of global warming. **He ordered the United States to pull out of the Kyoto Protocol which delayed implementation.** Hurricane Katrina led to the conclusion that the increase in numbers of severe storms and severity of them can clearly be attributed to global warming increasing the urgency to ratify the Kyoto Protocol.

One of the outcomes of the tragic 9/11 terrorist attack was the creation of the Department of Homeland Security which would integrate federal agencies such as Border Patrol, Immigration and Naturalization, Coast Guard, Secret Service, FEMA(Federal Emergency Management) and others. The objective of this reorganization was to protect our homeland against disasters including terrorist attack. That was a good action in principle. But the Bush Administration cut the budget for FEMA and many other federal programs thus diverting funds to the Iraq War substantially weakening programs previously  authorized to increase our protection.

Another example was cutting the FAA(Federal Aviation Authority) Research and Development budget by $400 million to divert those funds also to Iraq which already was costing the tax payer $200 billion and had mushroomed the federal deficit to historic high levels. This money was supposed to be used to improve the safety of our air traffic control system.

To head the Department of Homeland Security, a vast organization of hundreds of thousands employees, the president appointed a judge whose only management experience was the management of a court room. Making the leadership even more ineffective, he appointed an obscure lawyer from Oklahoma to head the critically important **FEMA** (Federal Emergency Management ) which has the responsibility for dealing with disasters across our nation. This person had little experience managing anything having been defeated when he ran for Congress and fired as head of the Arabian Horse Association.

After spending many billions of Dollars and nearly five years building the Homeland Security Department, should Americans feel safer? Of course. **Wrong!** When the National Hurricane Center issued dire warnings to evacuate New Orleans and activate emergency contingency plans to get ready for a killer Category 5 hurricane with sustained winds of 175 mph, all emergency resources in New Orleans, Louisiana and at the federal government should have gone into high gear and activated its emergency plans. Yes, one day before the storm hit and it headed directly for New Orleans which was warned of the potential of a levee break and huge disaster, its Mayor issued a mandatory evacuation order. Half of the population heeded it and fled the city the best way they could. But the other half stayed and one of the reasons was that New Orleans has a lot of poor people who can't afford to spend $30 to fill up their car, a bus or plane ticket and have no money for motels even if they could leave.

**There was a need for massive evacuation supported by the government at all levels and there was none.** The storm hit New Orleans as a Category 4 hurricane and some levees caved in letting the waters from Lake Pontchartrain flow and flood nearly the entire city while the torrential rains filled New Orleans below sea level basis with even more water which couldn't be pumped out because the pumps failed.

This became undisputable and tangible proof that the Corps of Engineer urgent proposal to upgrade the levee and pump system was indeed valid and the money should have been allocated. Residents unable to leave the city survived by climbing to roofs and  higher stories in their buildings while flood waters rose to over 15 feet. They improvised rafts to get to shelters or find boats. The Mayor issued an SOS pleading for federal help to save his citizens and provide drinkable water and emergency medical assistance.

The Superdome designated as an emergency shelter only for disabled became overrun with 20,000 people who had nowhere else to go. With no  water, no running toilets, no provisions or facilities and the roof partially fallen down during the storm, the great Superdome turned into a nightmarish stinking biohazard hell. The police became overwhelmed with looting and people concerned with self preservation, two police officers committed suicide and martial law was ordered as the governor dispatched whatever resources the State had available.

**Where was the President of the United States?** On vacation on his Texas ranch and then on to give a speech in California. Congress was in summer recess. The news media came in before any federal help and broadcast the horrors of the disaster for the world to see. Finally, the Federal government help started arriving five days after the storm had passed.

I personally saw CNN ask the FEMA Administrator where his organization was and he said he had just been informed the prior day and that was day four. The reporter further said that he would only need to turn on the TV and he would know all he needed to activate his people. He said he did see it on TV but needed "official notification".

As I write this chapter on September 5, Labor Day celebrating the "American Worker", the great City of New Orleans has been declared a bio hazard area with coast guard helicopters and military personnel on boats rescuing survivors to empty the city completely.

Refugees from New Orleans are finding their way into Texas, Arkansas, Florida, Georgia and other states to be with relatives, friends and into shelters many communities have set up. Refugees camps have been set up in Baton Rouge. The New Orleans Airport although open, has been turned into an emergency medical facility.

Casualty was estimated in the thousands as more bodies are found floating and in waterlogged buildings. One could see bodies laying in the streets. The majority of casualties were not from the wind or damaged buildings. The casualties are from drowning, starvation, disease, civil violence. A view of New Orleans on Labor Day, 2005, saw major fires throughout the downtown area as firemen are unable to deal with them for lack of water and means to fight the fires. They simply are allowed to burn themselves out.

This is New Orleans, not in a third world country. It is a major city in the United States of America, the strongest and most advanced country in the world. The Hurricane is an act of nature. The aftermath is the result of poor or lack of planning by government leaders at local, state and federal levels.

**The tragic aftermath was made far worse than it needed to be because of bad decisions all the way to the President.** The excessive loss of lives can be attributed especially to the delay in advance preparedness and failure by FEMA to immediately respond to the disaster. On the seventh day after the hurricane hit, the Mayor of New Orleans gave up his city to the federal and state authorities which finally came and reassigned the entire police department to a rehab and evaluation Center in Baton Rouge, the state capital 70 miles away.

The city rapidly become a disease infected cesspool not suitable for human occupancy and the question will arise whether to return the city to the Mississippi Delta Swamp it once long ago for the bayou people to again reign or rebuild the city.

By September 20, the FEMA head had resigned, a Coast Guard Admiral was put in charge of the Gulf Coast recovery and rebuilding which was estimated to cost $200 billion and finally, a qualified FEMA head had been appointed.

The people of New Orleans and the general Gulf area believed and assumed that their elected leaders responsibly managed their country and were safe. **They and the entire country were grossly misled and deceived into a false sense of security.** There was no Homeland Security for these people until it was too late for many and an entire city drowned.

This book is about honesty, truth and responsibility by the leaders of America's corporations and elected leaders and bringing the real story to the people. The American people deserve no less.

*"There is nothing more frightful than ignorance in action*

Johann Wolfgang von Goethe*"*

# America
# A Great Nation in Decline

*"When war is declared, truth is the first casualty "*
Arthur Ponsony

*"It is unwise to be too sure of one's own wisdom"*
Mahatma Gandhi

*"Division weakens, unity strengthens"*
Shirley Karger

**What made America a great country?** People from many different walks  coming together to live in one nation, work along side by side, become friends with one another and make new families together. This principle is what made America strong since the beginning. The "**cement**" which binds us all together is our interpersonal communications in one **common language**. The foundation to all this is our heritage from where we come. If the Germans, the Italians, the Russians, the French, Spanish and all people with so many different languages didn't learn one common language and adjust to one another in work, play and marriage, America as it is would not have happened.

What's happened over recent years is **contrary to the American way and reverses the trend toward greater unity among America's people.** Rather than adjusting to the American ways by adopting the common language which since the beginning was English, some people want Americans to adopt their language This has gradually been **dividing** rather than  uniting  the  people  resulting  in  a weaker America.

It is a trend spreading across America. Our founding fathers of 1776 would tell Washington that fraud is being committed against this great nation. Multilingual ballot and medical workers with poor English language skills spreading across much of the service sector are **increasingly deteriorating the quality of work** causing friction between people and increasingly leads to serious bodily harm when medical mistakes are made. I know because in 1993 while getting an angioplasty, I went into cardiac arrest when a nurse misunderstood the doctor's instructions due to a language problem. Miscommunication between pilots and control towers and among workers account for the majority of airplane crashes. There is a school in Miami teaching aviation English just for pilots and controllers to minimize this problem as English is the official language of the airways for safety reasons.

**The Iraq war and how it came to be** illustrates how America is slipping in stature and strength. This is measured not how we expand our influence through the force of war at gun point, but how well we communicate and negotiate with people of different cultures. This war first started out to punish a dictator not ruling to our standards. Then it evolved into a much longer than expected war with the purpose of enforcing a different way of life on a people who have lived their own way for thousands of years. I am not suggesting that our ways are better than theirs. Rather, it illustrates that the present administration takes to military force when diplomacy and other less destructive means fail. Eisenhower once said **"War is the failure of negotiations"** and **the Iraq war is an example of such failure**. History bears out this principle.

Our military effort to inject western democratic values in a region where these principles are foreign in concept relative to both religious and secular rule **are doomed to failure based on history**. Enforcing our radically different culture and ways of life onto other people just does not work.

This is evidenced nearly three years into this war as casualties on all sides are rising resulting from an emerging full blown civil war between the local Iraq religious factions. I predicted this in a report issued on May 1, 2003, the day President Bush landed on the aircraft carrier announcing the fall of Baghdad three months after the Iraq invasion was launched.

**The political power of religious fundamentalists and right wing conservatives emerged** during the past election. That accelerated the decline of our nation by amplifying the differences rather than the commonalities of our citizens. This is divisive rather than unifying and it's time we view this trend seriously. Why? Because this process is gradually shifting our nation toward a **theocracy** wherein moral principles based on a specific religion are beginning to impact our lives as elected government leaders increase their efforts to incorporate their personal religious based principles into secular laws.

**Medical research** is an area increasingly becoming inhibited by government restrictions founded on morality issues based on specific religious beliefs. **Embryonic Stem Cell research** became severely limited when the current administration issued an executive order prohibiting the use of federal funds for this type of medical research. The scientific community agrees that work in embryonic stem cell research could dramatically alleviate incurable diseases and reduce the human suffering of many patients. This scientific restriction set America back in one of the most promising biotechnology areas with many scientists in this field leaving the country to work where they are welcome to continue their research.

**These factors accelerate America's decline in world** leadership while the globalization of the economies continues to spread. Although I address the globalization of world economies in other chapters, I felt it is important to specifically focus on this in a chapter addressing America as a nation in decline thus defrauding citizens of the promise made by the nations founders.

# Is Theocracy Emerging In America?

**Theocracy:** A government of a state ruled by divine guidance and by officials who are regarded as divinely guided. A state where religious doctrine rules and is integrated into secular law.

Embryonic stem cell research is considered one of the leading emerging technologies that has significant potential to bring healing and long life to sufferers of disease and accident victims. The world's foremost medical scientists agree with this and the late Christopher Reeve was a superman testament to this potential. California committed billions of state funding toward this critical research even though it embarked on an austerity program to bring fiscal sanity to a nearly bankrupt state. Yet, George Bush, president of still the greatest nation in the world looked upon for leadership, publicly stated that he would veto any bill the Congress might pass to allow Federal funding of this vital and life saving technology. Why? Because using an embryo which would normally be discarded is like taking a life and that's against his religious belief.

This is the same president who immediately after being elected to his first term issued an executive directive canceling federal funding of family planning programs focused on the poor nations such as Africa which suffers from severe overpopulation and disease. These countries desperately need help in educating its poor and sick but our president says this is against his religious belief so he cut the funding for these programs. **Does this make sense to you? Is this the action of a great country?**

The presidential decisions were based on his religious beliefs and his **personal interpretation thereof**. They also reflect the belief and doctrine of powerful evangelistic groups who were principally responsible for gathering the votes in both elections to bring this president to power in America. One could ask the question about "**conflict of interest**" in this matter but we won't address that here.

More important is the question of the role of "**religious belief**" vested in the person who is head of state of the most powerful nation on Earth or for that matter, any person of authority and power over people from diverse ethnic and religious backgrounds. **This question is of extraordinary importance** because the foundation of the U.S. Constitution rests on the separation between "church and state".

Let's be clear about one thing. The founding fathers of this nation had deep personal beliefs based on Christian-Judaic principles. Over the years, government and judicial officials have painstakingly avoided making official rules based on **derivative interpretations of their personal religious beliefs.** There simply are too many variant interpretations for one person who happens to be in top authority to initiate rules based on what he believes is right and force, by his authority, his particular interpretations on all the people regardless of their individual personal beliefs.

One important American principle is to encourage all citizens to ask when they have questions about government affairs and for officials to accept that responsibility by **giving straightforward answers**. In recent years, a rising number of religious leaders have strongly encouraged their flock to consider the White House occupant to be a "man of God" and that what he says and directs is ordained by God.

These "followers" are also encouraged to accept the **word from the "White House" on the basis of faith** and that it may be un-American to question such word. This goes directly against the principles upon which America was founded because the founders came to this country to get away from countries governed by such principles.

When a head of government supported by one particular brand of religion initiates rules based on his religious belief, that's called "Shariah" by today's Islamists and "Doctrine" by the ruler of Spain during the Inquisition in the 15th Century.

Why am I addressing this issue in a book about corporate and government fraud? Because a country moving toward a less open society is moving into the direction of less disclosure, a more restrictive press and greater central control by not only the ruling party, **but the ruling inner circle.**

Evidence of this includes the punishment of CBS and Dan Rather resulting from the election coverage and the mid 2005 Newsweek coverage of prisoner treatment at Guantanamo Bay. Stories were aired and then pulled back with reporters punished. Interestingly, the very persons surfacing the stories somehow either changed their minds or recanted effectively pulling the rug from the news agencies. Concurrently, the White House press secretary said that news agencies should be more careful and that the punishment already meted out wasn't enough. Then, just a few weeks after the Newsweek reports and it received punishment from the White House, the general news media declared the American terrorist prison camp to be this century's "**Gulag**". If you don't remember what a "Gulag" was, they were the harsh prison labor camps in Siberia to which Stalin's political adversaries were sent.

**Months after CBS canned Dan Rather** from his news anchor job and assigned him to 60 Minutes Wednesday, that show was cancelled despite high ratings and just having received a Peabody Award.

Although this is 65 years later, this is remotely reminiscent of the **German propaganda machine** headed by Hitler's Propaganda Chief Josef Goebbels, who tightly controlled the German press. The Soviet Communism regime had an army of "cultural" monitors making sure officials at all levels "towed the official line" and ensured that few people dared ask questions about what was happening. The consequence asking the wrong questions could be fatal.

During times when rulers were also heads of the state religion any variant to state belief would be taken to task as heretics and face grave consequences and literally so. I am talking about today's Iran and Saudi Arabia. What do you think would happen to a priest who commented on an issue at variance with the Pope's doctrine on a specific issue?

During the Iraq war, it was considered un-American to raise questions despite it going badly and no weapons of mass destruction were found and intelligence that led us into that war was declared grossly deficient. A pastor ordered his congregants to vote for the Republican candidate or face expulsion from his church. Although eventually forced to resign about this, his action achieved the intended result. Their "man of God" was elected.

**A firestorm erupted in the Congress** during mid 2005 over ultra conservative presidential nominees for judicial posts. The fear was that personal religious interpretations by the proposed judges would alter the American landscape relative to the definition of when life begins and overturn of Roe vs Wade abortion law which gave women some say over their bodies.

The evangelistic interpretation of religion and its derivative moral values became a primary concern of many Americans because that issue decided the 2000 election and changed the course of world history. **The suppressive characteristics** of a regime too steeped in religion and its narrow interpretation can have a profound impact on a nation and its economy.

Corruption tends to flourish in countries where free speech is suppressed even a little and that's bad for most people and especially investors. While I am not saying that the United States government has become a theocracy, the administration under George Bush appears to have taken on some of its characteristics.

We all should be reminded that any country that allows its government to invoke the laws of its particular religion is doomed to eventually fail. **That's the lesson of history.** The purpose of including this commentary is only to stimulate objective thought on this subject.

## *"Individual freedom is precious"*
Shirley Karger

# National Security
# Vs
# Privacy and Freedom

Let's define what's important to national security and freedom to live as we chose.

**Security:** Freedom from danger, measures taken to prevent crime, attack or sabotage

**Privacy:** Freedom from unauthorized intrusion, state of being apart from observation

**Martial Law:** The suspension of civil law replaced by military law in the interest of national security

**Freedom:** absence of restraint

The *reichsführer* otherwise known as Adolph Hitler was delivering one of his *reichsprachen* telling his subjects what was good for them. The soldiers with red armbands and swastikas stood at attention. Tanks lined up while a large armored Mercedes convertible rolled in with Himmler and Ribbentrop who were Hitler's most important ministers responsible for state security and propaganda. **These people controlled what the people were told and enforced nearly total control over their lives.** I know this because **I was there in 1939** when my grandfather took me to the square in Berlin where this all was happening. In the name of state security, my entire family was uprooted, taken to a concentration camp and eventually all were killed and I was spared only because my parents sent me out of the country to live with strangers, foster homes and orphanages. This was an extreme example of a totalitarian state where all aspects of life were controlled by the state and I take it personally when freedom is threatened.

It's 1957 in **Budapest, Hungary** where the students revolted against the oppressive regime installed by the Soviet Union originally by Stalin when he "liberated" that country from the Hitlerian Germany. The people rejoiced thinking they were regaining their freedom but their joy was cut short when the Soviet tanks rolled in and squashed the cry for freedom. This was yet another example of how force is used to oppress people, squash their freedom and control their lives. Taking a step back 500 years takes us to Spain where people are forced to accept the state religion or face either death or expulsion from their country.

It's Washington in the early 50's when Senator Joseph McCarthy held hearings in the Capitol investigating communist infiltration into the media, film making and defense industries. Lists of suspected communists were compiled based often on no more than a "whisper" by someone who didn't like you. If you were on that list, you lost your security clearance and if you worked in the defense industry, it cost your job. If you were an actor and there were many in the film industry on that list, you lost your ability to get into the films because you were blackballed. That spread across our country to be remembered as "**The McCarthy Era**", McCarthyism and Orvellian because people were afraid to speak out for fear on just becoming a suspect.

Today, we have 9/11, the war on terrorism, Homeland Security Administration, a new Intelligence tsar and yes, we have the Patriot Act. This was passed by Congress shortly after the 9/11 tragedy giving broad powers to federal agencies to peep into our private lives with new arrest powers based on just suspicion of being involved with terrorists. A person suspected of just being affiliated with terrorists could be **arrested without notice**, taken to undisclosed places and denied the same due process of the law given to murderers.

Today in 2005, the Congress is considering giving federal agencies the power of monitoring what we read and what movies we see. This is all in the **name of national security**. People who ask searching questions about the Iraq War are labeled unpatriotic, liberals and anti Americans without good moral values.

Investigations conclusively revealed that American soldiers and civilian interrogators committed brutalities and torture against prisoners in an Iraq prison during 2004. Investigations clearly revealed that torture and aggressive interrogation techniques were used at the Abugraib prison in Iraq Guantanamo Bay prison camp in Cuba where people have been interred since the Afghanistan war and still haven't been accused of a crime. They simply are **suspected** of having knowledge about terrorists. A prominent national magazine reported this and got a "face slap" by the White House. This followed Dan Rather, anchor on Evening CBS news for a quarter of a century, being reassigned to another program which soon therafter was cancelled because he dared report a negative about the president during his second term re-election campaign.

**Deep Throat**, the secret leak of the Watergate scandal which forced Richard Nixon to resign the presidency in 1974 revealed himself in the summer of 2005. Mark Felt, at age 91 believed it was his responsibility to finally tell about how he as the second man in charge at the FBI helped the reporters tell the truth about a president who abused his powers to hush up a crime using his **special White House team**. After the disclosure, some called Felt a traitor while others said he is a national hero.

**The "Contra Affair"** of the Reagan presidency was about a similar cover up but President Reagan was sufficiently shielded by others who took the fall. Now we come to the **Terri Schiavo** case which was about a young lady who suffered a medical tragedy in 1991 and went into a brain dead vegetative state for the next 15 years. Her husband wanted to "pull the plug" to end it and allow him to go on living.

But the governor of Florida intervened on Terri's behalf declaring "**her**" a ward of the state. This process went all the way through the legal system to the U.S. Supreme Court which confirmed all the prior court decisions. Terry was brain dead in a permanent vegetative state. There was a swell of support to "**save Terri**" from evangelists across the country who established a round the clock vigil with hundreds of people praying outside Terri's hospice. The U.S. Congress went into special session passing "**Terri's Bill**" which ordered that she be brought to Washington to testify before the congress. Think about this. What would it mean to have a "person" in permanent vegetative state on life support testify in a full Congressional hearing? Reason prevailed and the local judge did not enforce the "**subpoena**" for a comatose Terri to go to Washington. The plug was finally pulled allowing what had become of Terri 15 years before to officially and naturally die.

The husband, in the interest of having all doubts laid to rest proving to the world that there was no hope for Terri to recover arranged an autopsy performed by a team of medical examiners. These examiners announced in June of 2005 that Terri was not only permanently brain dead, she had been blind for the 15 years in the coma state, could feel, sense or hear nothing and that any bodily movements anyone may have seen were bodily reflexes.

Even after this report was made public, the Florida governor ordered a special investigation by prosecutors to determine if Terri's husband had called 911 quickly enough when she suffered the medical episode 15 years before to determine possible criminal wrong doing and prosecution. This in my view deserves the **Nobel Prize for Privacy Invasion.** It illustrates the power of religious groups over top government officials. Without any doubt, this is grossly inconsistent with maintaining personal freedoms.

**What's good for national security is also good for preserving privacy and freedom.** A nation is more secure when the people feel more secure. They will respect the leaders more if their privacy is reasonably respected. Instilling fear in people breeds contempt of the leaders which eventually leads to disloyalty, greater security measures and even martial law under extreme cases. In today's environment of fear instilled by the "War on Terror" what do you think could happen if another 9/11 attack or worse still, an attempt to assassinate the President were made? We could face martial law in the name of national security with civil liberties suspended for all citizens. How would that be different than the former Soviet Union under Stalin, the Third Reich of Hitler or let's go to 2005, Cuba under Castro?

A far better way to address national security while preserving privacy and individual freedom would be to launch a priority program to secure our borders, having a national identity card for all residents, citizens and foreigners so that we know who is here and where everybody lives. Such a card could be used to gain 100% access to all modes of public transportation and public buildings. The second dimension of terrorist control would be to use the latest technology to monitor cargo containers coming into our ports, nuclear power plants and critical industrial facilities making them far safer than they are even four years after 9/11. These actions would severely restrict the opportunity for terrorists to operate in this country and dramatically increase our security.

That, more than anything, would increase public confidence in our leaders and nation. Moreover, it would gain the respect of other national leaders who likely would implement similar systems and procedures. **Would this not have been a better deterrent to terrorism** than invading Iraq costing thousands of lives, destroying a nation and spending $300 billion in the process with the result of seeing a rise in world terrorism and creating a raging civil war?

Such a policy would have fostered greater international cooperation in rooting out and controlling world terrorism, led to greater economic stimulus in the U.S. and abroad and probably an oil price of $15 per barrel less than we faced in 2005. The airline industry may not have been bankrupted nor would the auto industry be on the brink of financial disaster.

History has shown that education, open society and respect for privacy lead to better times for all while shutting out crime and terrorism. **That would be good for our nation and lead to a more secure world while respecting privacy and preserving personal freedom.**

*"Security is the priceless product of freedom"*
B.E. Hutchinson

# Prescription for Change

*"Unless acted upon by an external force, we continue in the same direction achieving the same results "* .

We need to see changes in how we think about public corporations to better serve the shareholders who indeed are the legal owners. The board of directors elected by shareholders must serve the shareholders who elect them, rather that the management which appoints them. Bankruptcy laws must be changed for corporations to reflect equity for the business owners. Our schools need to teach ethical conduct as required courses and we need to learn how and when to say no to the boss. In this section, I dare to say that we must keep religion out of government and return our government to the principles upon which our founders created our nation.

# Jail To The Kings

When President Richard Nixon arrived, the band struck up *"Hail to the Chief"* with the *"pomp and circumstance"* fitting a head of state. But **when he left the White House in disgrace in July 1974**, the only *pomp* was the wind from the helicopter with the famous last hand wave. Just two months later, Gerald Ford, the Vice President who had just been sworn in to succeed Nixon as President pardoned Nixon to avoid a continuation of a national scandal through an otherwise probable indictment, trial and jail for Nixon. When Nixon died in 1994, he was given a state funeral befitting a head of state remembered for the great accomplishments he made as president. Under his watch, he declared the Vietnam War unwinnable, simply withdrew our forces and ended the draft. He initiated dialogue with the Soviet Union that eventually led to the fall of that totalitarian state, opened the door to China which today has become a giant participant in world commerce and under his leadership, American astronauts set Man's first foot on the Moon thus starting interplanetary travel.

**When Michael Milken** strode into the room as "King of Bonds" during the 80's, people stood up in awe and respect because when "Michael spoke, money flowed". He was the person who helped many companies raise money to get started, go public and yes, he was well paid averaging $250 - $500 million per year. That was twenty years before Dick Grasso was booted out as Chairman of the New York Stock Exchange for dealing himself $135 million pay. Michael paid his debt via a 10 year jail sentence out of which he served only two years and paid over $500 million in fines and restitution.

However, he was able to keep nearly $1 Billion which he used after getting out of jail to fund important prostate cancer research to help find a cure for himself and today remains a financial guru giving advice to the business world.

Let's now go to the present in 2005 to see the parade of Kings who enter the prison portals. These were dragged through lengthy and well publicized trials so that there would be retribution on behalf of the people who lost Billions because of them. **This public spectable** could be compared with the extreme case of the young adulteress who was placed in a hole at the center of Kabul, Afghanistan and stoned to death by the religious fanatics called Talibans who then ruled that country just a few years ago. **The process of public retribution probably is more important** than the obscurity which comes to most felons after a few years in jail. The scene of Kenneth Lay being led into court with handcuffs between U.S. marshals will be remembered longer than the length of time he may serve if convicted.

**Martha Stewart** convicted of lying about her single misdeed of one insider stock transaction already had her trial, conviction, finished serving her few months sentence and is back out in business making tons of money. We should remember her as a person who did her misdeed at the wrong time when the public demanded retribution and she was an easy but high profile target. She didn't steal nor cook any corporate books nor did she cause any company to go bankrupt, destroy pensions or careers. **She was convicted for her arrogance and her poor timing of lying** to Congress. She denied insider trading at the very same time Kenneth Lay and Jeff Skilling who had just fallen as CEO and President of Enron were telling Congress '*We had no knowledge of what went on at Enron. "*

Before that fateful day November 29, 2001 when the Wall Street Journal ran the article *Running on Empty-Enron Faces Collapse*, Kenneth Lay, Enron's Chairman and CEO had been one of President Bush's biggest financial backers, donating nearly $2 million to his campaigns, being a frequent White House visitor and key adviser on energy policy. He was indicted July, 2004 on corporate fraud charges with trial scheduled to start January, 2006, five years after his transgressions came to light. **Jeff Skilling**, the former Enron president was indicted in February, 2004 on charges which could cost him $90 million in fines and lifetime in jail. As of this writing, his trial has not been set. Thus, we will likely see several years of public *spectable* dragging the Enron disaster in front of the public and likely to include appeals which could last years. Andrew Fastow and his wife Leah pleaded guilty under a deal to testify against his bosses. Leah already has completed her one year sentence and Fastow was given ten years.

**Adelphia** Cable founder **John Rigas** and his son, Timothy were convicted in the summer of 2004 for stealing billions of Dollars from publicly held Adelphia Cable and sentenced a year later in June 2005. They simply used the company treasury as their family piggy bank for personal investments and use. John Rigas, age 80 was sentenced to 15 years which at his age is a life sentence while his son, age 49 was sentenced to 20 years. **Worldcom founder Bernie Ebbers** was convicted in March 2005 of a massive $11 billion accounting fraud and sentenced to 25 years which for him was for life. But he may never see the inside of prison because the judge granted him bail pending his appeal which could take years. Scott Sullivan, Worldcom's Chief Financial Officer testified against his boss in a deal with federal prosecutors for a reduced sentence.

**Dennis Koslowski**, the **TYCO** CEO and his financial officer, Mark Swartz were convicted mid 2005 for stealing a massive $600 million from TYCO for their own personal use. This trial followed a previous mistrial. Their raid on the Tyco bank account were for expensive paintings, high priced condos and the notorious $2 million birthday party for Koslowski's wife with a "Roman party" in Italy. For all this, were sentenced late September, 2005, to serve a minimum 8 years and pay combined more than $200 million restitution.

**Frank Quattrone,** the king of investment banking at Credit Swiss First Boston who made $120 million per year recommending stocks went to trial in 2003 which ended in a hung jury. He was finally convicted in a second trial early 2004 and sentenced to 18 months in jail. Quattrone as of fall of 2005 remains out on bail appealing his conviction. He was convicted for misleading investors and telling office people to destroy incriminating emails. During his reign, he was the unquestioned "*King of Research*" in the world of high tech stocks. When Frank spoke, stocks roared like a lion heard all the way to the mountain of gold from which Frank eventually fell in the Internet avalanche burying investors along its track.

Perhaps the greater crime are all those CEO's and top corporate officers who committed fraud against their employees, shareholders, customers and suppliers **but were never even charged.** Worse still is the lack of oversight by the boards which are supposed to oversee management on behalf of the shareholders. We should not forget the role of federal regulators such as the SEC which is supposed to prevent these types of disasters in public companies. **Was the SEC asleep or just looking the other way all those years?**

While sending a few of these deposed former corporate kings to jail with stiff sentences and dragging their process through the street of retribution may cleanse America's corporate soul for awhile, **Corporate America needs nothing short of a restructuring of the supervisory system**. We need reforms ensuring that management doesn't forget the shareholders who are the owners, provided the money to start the companies and grow them over the years. Read on to find out what changes I believe are needed.

*"Nothing so needs reforming as other people's habits"*

Mark Twain

# Reform
# The Board of Directors

*"If you want to fail in business, do it like the government does"* is an expression subscribed to by most astute business people. Government operations are usually far more inefficient than those of the private business world. Governments at all levels, Federal, state and municipal apply  Parkinson's Law of Economics which prescribes to **"spend whatever you raise in taxes and then some".** If business followed that "law", bankruptcy would be the norm with chaos and the extinction of the system as we know it.

But I am here to tell you that there is one area of government from which we have a lot to learn and that's **how our government is governed.** The basic principle of our Constitution is to provide a *"government of, by and for the people"* providing three branches of government which are the executive, judicial and legislative. The **Executive** department is lead by the President who is elected by the people. He directs and manages the affairs of the country in principle just principle like the president of a company does. The **Legislative** department is headed by the Congress which establishes the laws of the country and oversees the executive branch making sure that the President and his administration follow the strategy and policies established by the Congress which represents the people. The Congress serves a similar role in government as the Board does in industry. That role is called **oversight.** The **Judicial Branch** enforces the laws established by the congress while the Supreme Court arbitrates conflicts in the laws making sure they adhere to the Constitution.

The **people** of the United States of America own the government as specified by the principle, "A government of and by the people" and pay for its operations by paying taxes which add to the revenues generated by the government which "sells" many services paid for by users of such services. The people elect congressmen and senators who are placed there to **serve their best interest. We vote for someone else in the next election if we don't think they serve our interests properly.**

This process is the congressional elections which include campaign speeches, lots of handshaking and in recent years, massive communications via radio, TV, Internet and emails. After the elections, communications continue via newsletters, personal local appearances by the elected officials and their policy to invite concerns and complaints we have about what the executive branch is doing or failing to do.

**A publicly owned corporation can be compared in some respect with the government.** A publicly owned corporation is owned by the shareholders who are the equity owners of the business. They paid the original capital which established the business and on occasion are asked for more money when the revenues generated by the business aren't enough to support the business needs and cannot be met by borrowing from the banks. The corporation holds an annual election during which the management presents people to be elected or re-elected to the Board of Directors which oversees the company's management. This board establishes the broad policies for the company and **is supposed to oversee management to ensure those policies are followed and corporate objectives are achieved.** It has the authority to fire the president and hire a replacement. The Congress cannot hire the nation's president but through a difficult impeachment process, it can fire the President.

**What does any of this have to do with public corporations? Plenty.** The Board of directors of a public corporation legally represents the shareholders **and are elected by the shareholders.** Why is it that we rarely hear about the board? The only time we are even told about the existence of a board is when the company sends out its annual "Proxy" statement calling for the board's election at the annual meeting. Typically, the only reference to the board is a brief one paragraph giving the name of the person to be elected or re-elected and a few sentence bio.

There is no campaign to solicit your vote as is the case in government elections. There is not even an address, telephone number or email address where you can reach the person who is asking for your vote. In fact, the company typically goes through great pains in **hiding the whereabouts of the directors.** When a persistent shareholder finally locates the director, he typically will not return calls, emails or letters. The company instructs you to direct any communications to the Board via the company or its attorney. Never directly to the board members. When you do write, you rarely get any response at all or if you are lucky, a form letter saying nothing of substance. Most shareholder don't even know who the board members are, what they do nor do they seem to care.

The recently enacted Sarbanes Oxley legislation tried to make the board more accessible to shareholders. This new law requires a statement in the Annual Report and on the company website under Corporate Governance giving the procedure whereby shareholders may communicate with board members they elected. This typically is the name and address to the corporate attorney to which all communications must be directed and who will forward your communication or the essence of it to the board member you have addressed. Any response will of course also come through this law firm and you can bet such response is sanitized.

**There is plenty wrong with this picture.** We shareholders elect people about who we don't know much about to oversee the companies we own. These people set the policies and oversee the management of the companies we invest our hard earned Dollars in. We have no practical way to communicate with them. We can't do anything about it when they mismanage our companies and there has been plenty of that as we have learned over the past few years. About the only recourse we have is to hire class action lawyers to sue the management and the board but that usually accomplishes little. The key executives and board members are protected by insurance called "Errors and Omissions Insurance" whereby the company pays a premium to an insurance company which then pays out the money when the lawyers and company inevitable settle. **There are few if any consequences to the board for misdeeds, mismanagement and for the most part doing nothing.**

The real picture here is that the CEO typically selects the board member who for the most part becomes a person occupying a seat in a board room for which he gets paid per meeting plus either free stock or cheap options. Board members typically don't have a real investment in the company they serve and by real investment, I mean cash out of their own pocket. That's how it is and that's how the Enrons, Worldcoms, Adelphias and all that was covered in this book and you haven't even heard about came about. It was the Worldcom board which approved the $400 million loan to Bernie Ebbers to pay his titanic size margin call. It was the Enron board which claimed to know nothing about what was going on. The Montana Power board allowed the transformation of a great financially strong company into a high risk venture which led to liquidation and loss to all shareholders and employees.

It was the board of **Wireless** which approved the sale of its business via the bankruptcy court to the CEO's brother-in-law wiping out all shareholders and giving unsecured creditors 3 Cents on the Dollar. How many board members have even been indicted? I haven't ever heard of any. Have you?

**Whose interest were the directors of these boards serving?** By what we have seen, it for sure wasn't the shareholders and that's us. Yet, we are the ones who legally own these corporations via our shares. The term *shareholder* means simply that the money we invest via purchasing shares in the company gives the shareholder a percentage of ownership. Therefore, all shareholders own 100% of the company and yet, we seem to have so little to say about our company and yes, **it really is our company. Don't you ever forget that!** The only practical action we can take is to sell our shares. But that's not a good answer because we'll have the same problem in the next company we invest in.

**The problem is the system** and I am here to tell you that it needs to be changed. Moreover, I'll tell you how we should change it. There is something to be learned by looking at how our government oversees the executive branch and the President's performance. Admittedly, in my view, the performance in the White House has been miserable lately. But, there are plenty of communications about this miserable performance and we have the option to elect new people in the next election. We can demonstrate in front of the White House, write articles, sign petitions and in extreme cases, even riot. Have you ever heard of demonstrations in front of a corporate Hq or shareholder petitions against any CEO?

We need and in fact must **change the system. We must restructure the board of directors system making it responsive to the owners by serving the owners, rather than the top management.**

We need to have the Board sit on the same side as the owners whether they be us individual shareholders or large institutions holding huge blocks of shares. I rather have a crook on the board than a super honest person but incompetent executive so long as we sit on the same side and have common interest. That leads to my first change in corporate governance. The **following key elements** should be a part of board governance of all public corporations:

- Meaningful personal investment by each director
- Directors must be capable, not just figureheads
- Meaningful Communications with shareholders
- Shareholders must be meaningfully represented

**Each director must have a meaningful personal investment in the company.** That plainly means that he must have taken money out of his own pocket and invested in the same class of shares as we, the outside shareholders own. This excludes options granted for serving on the board or outright shares awarded as part of compensation. **It has to be cash out of his pocket** and it has to be meaningful relative to his or her net worth. The key element in this requirement is **risk. The director must have the same risk as we outside shareholders have.** We must share in the risk as well as the potential reward. This places us on the same side of the board table and can dramatically alter the board member's interest in what's happening. If the Enron directors had a meaningful investment into Enron stock with their own personal cash, I guarantee that their chorus would not have sung "*I didn't know*".

**Capable persons must serve on the board.** It isn't enough to be a tennis or movie star famous worldwide. The board member should know something about the business, its industry and the world of finance.

Hire the tennis or movie star as the company's spokesperson doing public relations. Don't hire such a person to entrust with the oversight of a Billion Dollar corporation. The board must have expertise in finance and the business world applicable to the company.

**The Board must be allowed to communicate with its constituents and that's us, shareholders,** just like our elected representatives to Washington do. This can be done very simply by making the board responsible for most shareholder communications such as financial releases and major corporate announcements. This function often called *nvestor relations* which is typically assigned to the Chief Financial Officer. The company should transfer this function to the board  to create the office of "**Shareholder Relations**" through which all significant shareholder and investor communications must flow. This structure would require the board to be very familiar with what's going on. The board would have to become involved with preventing problems before they get serious and be in the position of taking advantage of opportunities which otherwise might have gone by the wayside.

This office, reporting to a board member, would be responsible for all incoming shareholder communications and of course, observe the SEC fair disclosure rules. I am proposing to do no more or less than is typically done today. **The principal change is that the interface between the shareholder and the company is the Board, rather than the chief financial officer or the company attorney.**

**Finally, shareholders must be meaningfully represented on the board.** Under the present system, the CEO often selects the directors who are presented to the shareholders for election at the Annual Meeting. While there may be a board nominating committee, the board needs to actively nominate people who truly represent shareholders.

Typically, shareholders only learn about the new directors when a short bio is included in the Proxy Statement along with the statement that "management recommends a vote for the directors presented". I propose that the nominating committee be allowed to receive nominations from shareholders and that a process be established whereby shareholders are able to nominate directors. This is standard in any organization following Roberts Rules of Order and at least a semblance of this should be part of a corporate nomination process. The absence of this results in a board without independent directors with all nominees controlled by the CEO.

**The restructuring** I propose is simple, requires little changes to laws and can be done quickly. Maybe it takes a shareholder revolution to effect these simple changes. Maybe it's time you e-mailed your questions and concerns to management. Maybe you should pick up the phone to at least try calling the CEO. You could also write the SEC and when you see something looking illegal, contact the police. When all else fails, you could even call the reporter in the local paper and give management bad press, something which will really wake up management. They hate seeing their names in print in anything other than glory.

*"The board of directors must serve the interest and be responsible to the shareholders who own the business"*
Gunther Karger

# Shareholders Bill of Rights

There are well over 100,000 publicly held companies trading on the various exchanges such as NYSE, Nasdaq, Pink Sheets and that's just in the United States. Millions of people own stock in the public companies either directly by buying the shares on an exchange or via mutual funds or pension programs. The SEC(Securities and Exchange Commission) of the government oversees the industry with the National Association of Securities Dealers(NASD) appointed as the industry's self regulating agency licensing all brokers and ensuring they are in compliance with all the regulations. Despite these, the shareholders have been taking a beating for years and especially in recent years. Shareholders have lost billions and maybe even trillions in just the past five years considering the Internet Bubble, Telecom Meltdown, Enron/ Worldcom and all the companies where stocks went from over $100 to sub pennies. There is no question that the shareholders have been the bag holders and that bag has been filled with rotten dirt.

It's time for the creation of a **Shareholder's Bill of Rights which should be done right now.** Since there is no Constitutional Convention which wrote the Bill of Rights for the people of the United States, **I'll just get to it and do it in this book and here it is.**

# Shareholder Bill of Rights

**Whereas** we are shareholders who worked hard to save our money which we invest into public companies and

**Whereas** we are the shareholders of these companies who own them via the shares we purchased, we have important rights to which we are morally, legally and ethically entitled.

*Now therefore,* we declare and demand that:

- Management tells the truth in a timely manner
- Management works fulltime
- Management avoid conflict of interests
- Management respects shareholders as owners
- Management not use company money and resources for personal use
- Management and board members purchase shares with personal cash over and beyond any shares obtained via grants or options
- Management uses option grants for long term investment in the company and not sell stock at the time of exercise except sufficient shares to pay for the options cost
- Management gives prompt and respectful response to shareholder communications
- The board of directors represent the shareholders as owners of the business
- Management gives priority and reasonable attention to shareholder values as allowed by security law

# Reform Corporate Bankruptcy Law

*Bankruptcy: failure and impoverishment, hopelessly unable to pay debts; financial restructure under court protection and supervision*

During the old days, people who couldn't pay their debts were hauled to jail foreclosing any possibility of them ever paying what they owed. Bankruptcy laws were enacted to make it possible for people and businesses in a disastrous financial situation to make a fresh start and become a potential asset to society instead of being stuck forever in the quicksand of public liability. This gave individuals the chance to once again become taxpaying members of society while offering businesses the opportunity to reorganize from a failure to a successful enterprise.

In the eyes of the law, a corporation is a "**legal person**" with a name, a tax number and responsibilities to its family(employees and customers) and the community. Just like a person who has a house, car, furniture, investments, bank deposits, so does the corporation in its buildings, machinery, business goodwill, investments and bank deposits. While the individual owns all his or her assets, so does the corporation. However, while the person is a human being who can leave his assets to surviving family members or others via a will, the public corporation is owned by **shareholders** who bought their stake in the business by buying stock.

Unlike the individual who manages his family and personal assets directly, the shareholders are represented by a board of directors who hire the people to run the company and supervise them. But the shareholders remain the owners.

They are the people who put up the original money when the company went "public" and took the risk investing their money and trusting the managers of the corporation. Of course, board members, company managers and employees can also be shareholders.

**Bankruptcy laws are enacted to protect the owners** from creditors seizing their property which they in turn would sell to recover their debt. The principle of bankruptcy law is to enable a person to restructure his financial life under the protection of the bankruptcy court and to give everyone a fair chance to recover what's possible, given the debtor's circumstances without leaving him totally broke, destitute without home or means to support himself and his family. In a personal bankruptcy, the person generally gets to keep his home so he has a place to live, a car so he can get to work and support himself and his family and a minimum amount of money for food and life necessities.

Why is it that the shareholders, **the owners of the corporations, under present bankruptcy laws, usually lose everything with the creditors getting all?** A typical reorganization plan under present bankruptcy issues new shares to the creditors and selected key managers while canceling the stock leaving the original shareholder nothing. An alternative and often **favorite plan in the bankruptcy** of a small to medium sized company is to arrange for another company to purchase the operating assets, without any obligations, for an agreed upon price. The bankrupt company then is left only with the cash from the purchase which pays the creditors and bankruptcy expenses. The bankruptcy court then declares the stock cancelled and worthless leaving the owners, the shareholders absolutely nothing. **Is this fair? No!**

**This is just like stealing the home from an individual** or his savings which he placed into the stock for his retirement leaving him nothing. Refer to the chapter "*Is Chapter 11 a license to steal?*" for an actual case where this happened. You should know this is standard practice because that's how the bankruptcy system in the U.S. is structured.

**This is wrong, unfair and it's time shareholders stood up to the Congress and demanded a change.** Shareholders, as true owners of the corporation, the "legal person" for the publicly held business, should have the same rights as the individual going bankrupt. Just as the individual is given a basic home, a car to drive to work and money for food with the rest to pay the creditors, the **shareholders should be allowed to retain at least a token minimum ownership position in the new company** . That would enable them to participate in the future of the company, even if it's a much smaller equity position than before. Realistically, the shareholder would understand that there would be major dilution resulting from the transfer of debt into new equity. But, a total shareholder wipeout via share cancellation is just out and out grand larceny.

**Making this "crime" even worse,** this process is written into the present bankruptcy laws and supported by the Justice Department which manages the Bankruptcy Court System. The bankruptcy laws should also be revised to make it significantly more difficult for corporate managers to use the bankruptcy process to take a company private by simply having the shareholders wiped out. There should be written into the bankruptcy laws a provision requiring the "estate" and the buyers of the company to pay something also to the shareholders. After all, they are the owners. The present laws specify that shareholders get only what's left over after the creditors get paid 100 Cents of the Dollar and that means there rarely is anything left over for the shareholder.

There should be a provision which allocates something to the shareholder by reducing the "cents on the Dollar" allocation to the creditors.

**What should be done to resolve this grossly unfair situation?** The banks lobbied Congress and eventually won to water down the personal bankruptcy benefits to individuals by mortgaging the individuals future income. Shareholders should lobby Congress to change the corporate bankruptcy laws making them fairer to the investors. Unfortunately, we shareholders don't have the backing of the big banks and credit card issuers. But we do have the power of not re-electing our congressional and senate representatives. Thanks to the power of modern communications, **we also have the means of making a massive public stink embarrassing our Washington leaders**.

The corporate managers and lenders would probably be strongly against any such legislation on the basis that this would increase their risk. The flip side of this objection is that corporations would be able to raise more capital by issuing more stock as shareholders would be less nervous about potential bankruptcy where they lose it all. That would reduce the need for borrowing from lenders while encouraging institutional investors to invest more in the companies.

The last reform is about management. **The bankruptcy laws should require the installation of either a new CEO or an interim CEO as part of any reorganization plan.** The CEO who led the company into bankruptcy should not be allowed to continue because part of the **fresh start** should be fresh management. This is no less important than purging a cancer ridden body of its bad cells to prevent return of the disease.

*Shareholders, it's time you insist that you get your fair share, even in corporate bankruptcy!*

# Teach Ethical Conduct in School

**Ethical conduct:** the discipline dealing with what is good and bad and with moral duty and obligation

**Moral behavior:** conforming to a standard of right behavior

**Ethics and morality** usually are things addressed by clergy in churches and temples. Bible classes are full of references to chapter, verse and line giving explanation of what's happening in our daily lives. That's where it usually ends. When we leave those places and events, we go back to our daily lives usually forgetting what we just discussed and do what we did before in the way we are used to doing it. Those are abstract things not usually relevant to our daily lives.

**This couldn't be more wrong.** Ethical conduct is what drives how we manage our lives both personally and in business. The way we relate and work with people determines success or failure in our personal lives and business. Sure, you might say that ethics and moral issues are based on religious principles and that's a private matter. That's true. What we need to do however is to extract from the religious aspect those things which deal with real life issues to help us make choices between right and wrong.

For example, *"Thou shall not steal", "Thou shall not kill" and "Thou shall not lie"* come from the "Ten Commandments which is fundamental to Judeo-Christian religions and yes, even Islam. These principles are embedded into civil laws enacted by governments throughout the world since the beginning of time and have real earthly and very serious meaning. Killing someone is committing murder and you can get a death sentence for that.

Lying is perjury and you go to jail or worse still, you get your tongue cut out if you live in a fundamentalist Islamic country. If you steal, you better not live in a country ruled by Islamic law because you might get your hand cut off. When the Taliban ruled Afghanistan, women were stoned to death for even suspecting committing adultery. Here, you have a fight with your spouse and might get divorced. Indeed, these universally biblical derived moral and ethical principles have serious earthly meaning.

This book is about right and wrong in business and the **consequences of choosing the wrong side**. Bernie Ebbers who got a 25 year jail sentence picked the wrong and unethical solution to resolve serious business problems at Worldcom. He didn't mean to break any laws. But he robbed the pockets of many shareholders, destroyed the careers of thousands of employees and ended Worldcom which could have remained as a leading telecommunications company. When Ebbers instructed his chief financial officer to do whatever was necessary to increase the earnings, Scott Sullivan cooked the books by moving expenses to become capital investments. That was the wrong road to take. **A better and ethical path** would have been to tell Ebbers that it was time to reduce expenses and digest the growth the company had over recent years and yes, maybe even sell off a few business operations.

Yes, the same applies to even Enron. Instead of creating those offshore partnerships to hide the liabilities from the balance sheet, Andrew Fastow should have told Kenneth Lay, his boss and CEO, that it is time to restructure Enron by stopping further acquisitions and write down some existing assets to their real value.

Sure, Enron stock might have crashed and some employees may have been laid off. But, Enron would have survived to glow in the sunshine another day with the stock recovering and employees pensions there when they retire.

**Before we get out of this kitchen of cooked gooses,** let's not forget Martha Stewart. She was not convicted of that famous single stock trade of selling 4000 shares on Imclone because of inside information from her friend. She was convicted of **lying on the witness stand** about it and that's perjury which is a criminal offense . She preferred to lie rather than admit having made a mistake and simply pay a fine. Another bad decision based on taking the wrong road of ethics.

**So what should be done to correct this problem?** It's really quite simple. Teach ethics in school and I mean school at all levels including high school, college and graduate schools. Ethics should especially be a required course in graduate business schools. Some already are doing it and that's good. But it should be required to graduate and not be an elective.

Hey, we can't do that, says the chorus of ultra liberal activists. We can't have any such teaching in public schools because religion must be kept out of schools and government. I agree with the principle of separation of "Church and State". That doesn't mean we can't develop courses focused strictly on ethical values common to most religions. These are really simple common sense things and would address those aspects already adopted by the civil and criminal legal system of most countries.

There is no reason the principles of ethical issues involving stealing, lying and other obvious crimes cannot be addressed in non religious terms and focusing on earthly laws well known to everyone. Young people need to be given the history about what happens when unethical paths are taken solving business problems and be given alternative methods of dealing with them.

School is one place for this, just as school is the place to learn math, how to design buildings and to become a doctor. A curriculum can be designed to focus on the real and essential ethical issues.

There is no need for prayers in the classroom, references to biblical passages or traditions based on specific religions to achieve this. That controversial issue can and should be avoided. The focus should be on the issues relevant to behavior and decision making at our jobs and in business. Students need to be told in a professional clear and unemotional manner about what's right and wrong relative to acceptable practices and the **earthly consequences** of ignoring doing "what feels right" and doing "what feels wrong". Trust your gut feeling. **When it doesn't feel right, don't do it.**

# Practice honesty
# or
# face the consequences

# When to Tell Your Boss No!

**Boss:** A person who exercises control or authority; one who directs or supervises workers; master

**NO:** Act of refusing, denial, a vote against

    The boss tells you to take a week's trip on a new assignment but your wife tells you to stay home to finish up your house painting. You don't feel well and think it's a mistake to leave town away from your doctors. A federal regulation says that the assignment your boss gave you may not be legal.

    **Who is the boss here?** You have to pick between your boss, your wife and your body which is yourself. Regardless of whose directive you take, you take a risk.

    Let's get real. I was told by my boss, the president of the company, to issue a financial release which clearly violated federal accounting regulations. I refused which led to my giving up a high paying job. He issued that press release himself and for that, he eventually was sent to went to jail and the company went bankrupt. Another time, I was directed to raise my revenue forecast to hide reality from the banks who lent the money to the company. I refused to "cook the books" and eventually was laid off. The boss changed my numbers and the company within a few years went bankrupt and out of business (Eastern Airlines).

    Field Marshall Ervin Rommel, the famous "Desert Fox" general who conquered North Africa for Hitler eventually went against his boss, Adolf Hitler and ended up dead on a German roadside but was given the funeral of a national hero and is remembered as a brilliant general instead of a Nazi criminal.

The Nazi soldier rounds up innocent Jewish civilians from their house in the dead of the night, puts them on a truck scheduled to meet with a cattle train bound for a mass killing factory where on arrival they are stripped, gassed and cremated. (This actually happened to my parents). He obeyed his order, lived to survive the war but his country was destroyed along with most of his bosses. Corrie Ten Boom, a Christian woman in Holland hid people who somehow escaped the Gestapo and saved many lives during World War II. She and her family were caught doing what was forbidden and her family was imprisoned. Corrie's boss was her conscience which she followed, instead of the laws of her country at that time. While she and her family suffered, her conscience prevailed as she died at age 91 in 1983 but the German Third Reich crumbled into ruins in 1945.

Scott Sullivan, Worldcom's Chief Financial Officer did what his boss Bernie Ebbers told him to do even though he knew it was illegal. He cooked the books making the earnings look a lot better than they really were. In doing this, Scott ignored his other boss **who were the shareholders and the real owners of Worldcom**. A financial officer is a person who has legal responsibility to the owners for accurate reporting, even if it means to go against the CEO.

A lawyer must maintain confidential all information relevant to the case or face disbarment. That's a sacred tradition within the legal community and universally respected even by judges. A lawyer's client is his boss, period. Except for a situation when the lawyer comes into information which if not communicated to the police may result in an imminent serious crime such as murder. In such a case, even the lawyer may shift his boss from client to the police.

**What's the bottom line**? Not only does there come a time to say NO to your boss. There also comes a time when you have to **decide who is the real boss** relative to the decision or action you are about to take.

If you are a janitor told to mop up the floor in the back room, you do it without question. Right? Maybe not if the floor you are told to sweep is full of fresh blood. Maybe you call the police instead.

Saying no to the boss is one of the most difficult things a person may be led to do. But it goes more fundamental than that. "**No**" is just not in our psyche. It's a lot harder to say "no" to a child throwing a tantrum than just letting it have what it wants to keep it quiet. The first choice helps the child face life's realities and succeeds. The other may ruin the child for life by denying it the conditioning we all need in our early years.

**What's the answer?** How do you know when you must say no and risk consequences? This is the time to honestly consider the options of saying yes or no and the consequences either way. **Focus on the potential probable consequences and you will find the right answer.**

*"The right thing*
*is not always the easiest but the hardest*
*choice may be your best"*

# Reform the Health System

Why am I including America's health system in a book on corporate and government fraud? **Because it belongs**. The combined might of America's health industry and government could today deliver a vastly improved medical system in a far more cost effective way than it does. That's fraud because it robs us not only of lots of money, but more importantly, it denies us better quality of life and increased longevity. **Medical fraud** is rampant across the entire health system. It adds to the high insurance premiums which are so high that an estimated more than 40 million Americans go without it because they can't afford it or simply can't get it.

There is **criminal fraud reaching in the billions** and people do go to jail. Medical providers including doctors, hospital administrators, medical supply companies and pharmacies are caught with all kinds of schemes. Unfortunately though, only a small number of them get caught. Just look at what happened to me.

I learned by accident that a medical supply company was billing Medicare $577 per month for an invalid motorized bed for me for over a half year racking up a $3500 bill. But I am thankfully not an invalid, never asked for the device nor had I ever heard of the medical supply company sending the bills, using my personal data inclusive of my Social Security Number. Even after reporting this to the local police and the FBI, the bills continued coming months after I reported this crime.

Medicare alone accounts for $142 billion in the 2006 federal budget and that doesn't include the estimated $560 million additional needed over the next ten years to pay for the prescription benefit becoming effective in 2006. Americans spent an estimated $5.6 trillion in 2004 for health care. **That's a lot to protect from fraud.**

Here and now, I'll focus on what can and should be done to dramatically reduce medical fraud while significantly improving the health care system and lower costs. I will address several major areas where we could achieve meaningful improvement. These are, technology, drugs, Medicare, insurance and legal.

**Technology** is the area where so much more can be done using just what's available today. There is no excuse for the **administrative nightmare** patients and providers are forced to endure. All patient records should by now be in computer files updatable nearly without significant cost. There is no excuse why patients should be given forms to fill out multiple times giving their names and other static information to the doctor they have seen for years or clinics or hospitals they have been to in the past. Every time a patient fills out one form, someone in the doctors office has to handle it, file it or update the office records.

This is a tremendous duplication costing big time and slowing down the real business the office should be in and that's to provide health care. There is no excuse why this records updating process couldn't be handled routinely by **e-mail** and done only when there is a change thus avoiding a mountain of unnecessary duplicate paperwork.

**Referrals by primary care physicians** to specialists often force a patient to needlessly visit the office and can take weeks to get. Sometimes, the patient dies before the referral is issued. This could easily be handled by an e-mail to the office and reviewed either by staff or doctor who then could issue it to the patient via an e-mail form. The office would need less administrative clerks and the doctor may see patients less frequently leading to reduced fees from routine office visits.

Offsetting this, the doctor could easily be paid for this service by calling it an "**e-visit**" and charging a fee and increase the fees per visit as he can spend more quality time with the patients.

This fee could be covered by the insurance company, included within an HMO or subject to a patient co-payment charged to the patient's credit card on a pre-approved basis. Minor medical problems could also be handled via **e-visits** reducing the need for excessive office visits. Such office visits could even cause medical problems due to exposure to patients with communicable diseases in the waiting room. The **e-visits** reduces the time an employee has to be absent from work and that's a big benefit to both employee and employer. Doctors could spend more quality time with patients preventing disease which would reduce hospital visits and unnecessary diagnostic tests. These simple things alone could save Billions in cost while improving the quality of health care. This is nothing which could not be implemented today. There is no excuse why we don't already have it.

**More advanced technology** is available for hospitals to dramatically reduce costs while also improving medical outcomes. For example, **telemedicine** monitoring patients from central locations staffed by critical care doctors reduce the need for nurses to administer routine checks such as blood pressure and other minor diagnostic tests.

These systems, already finally finding their ways into some hospitals, reduce or even eliminate the need for patients to wait which results in better outcomes and less suffering. The central monitor staff detects the coming of a medical emergency or painful episode before the patient even starts to experience it. The floor monitor then sends a nurse or doctor to initiate the proper medical procedure or administer medication. Telemedicine systems are already being implemented in critical care hospital areas but should be expanded to all hospital beds.

**Telemedicine networks** should also be deployed by doctors connecting them with diagnostic clinics so they can immediately know what's happening to patients while undergoing tests and even order additional tests. Dramatic cost and health care benefits would result.

**The drug** area of health care is a disaster adding huge costs to the health system. Drug costs have soared to unsustainable levels. People now have to make decisions between food and drugs. Insurance companies prevent patients from taking some drugs even though their doctors prescribe them because they aren't on the formulary list which is based on cost. Some patients get their drugs from outside the United States via mail order pharmacies in Canada and elsewhere. Some travel to get their medicines. Others go to the health food store and buy herbs, minerals and other remedies not regulated by the drug industry thinking they may work as well.

**The solution is really simple.** The American buying drugs at the local drug store gets the same drug as the Canadian or anyone in most countries get. While there always are cost differences in various locations based on transportation costs and local economies, the dramatic variance between what the American is forced to pay and the person elsewhere is unjustified.

What we have here is **a price fixing system mandated allowed by the U.S. Government**. The recent Medicare Prescription Act specifically made it illegal for the Medicare Administration to negotiate drug prices. Suddenly, the drug prices jump up dramatically. That's price fixing and illegal in other industries. Just reforming this practice allowing drug prices to be set by market forces would dramatically reduce health care costs while improving the quality of health care. The solution to this problem is political.

But as we all know, the industry maintains an extraordinary lobby in Washington and thus, Congress gets paid off with us folk footing the bill in higher medical costs and lower than possible health care quality. That's fraud in any language and without any doubt belongs in this book. Paying $15 per pill which cost 15 Cents to manufacture is simply a raid on our wallet with a gun pointed to our heads with the robber saying " *Pay or die.*"

Medicare is probably the most fraud ridden system in American business. It's designed for fraud. When a medical supply company can bill Medicare for an invalid motorized bed for a patient not sick and who walks two miles a day, takes daily exercises and maintains a half acre full of tropical trees, (me) that's fraud. When a system allows a provider of medical service to get a patient's Social Security and other personal data without any knowledge by the patient, that's identity theft. When a doctor can send a bill to Medicare for 5 visits to a patient's hospital bed but only scanned the chart provided by the hospital and not even speaking once to the patient, that's overbilling and definitely fraud. When the hospital bills Medicare for toilet paper allocated to patients as part of the overall hospital supplies while charging patients $900 per day for the room, that's gouging.

I have seen cases where a post office box is used as a "clinic address" used by people who don't even speak English and criminally use that "phantom" office as a medical supply company billing Medicare for undelivered equipment. This fraudulent billing to Medicare is a huge industry and means that enough of the bills get paid before law enforcement officers close them down. The system has become a cash cow at the tax payers and patients' expense.

**How can we dramatically reduce Medicare fraud?** It's simple. We just have to adopt the system already in place for the non Medicare system. Every procedure must be approved by medical professional familiar with the patient. Severe penalties should be given to any medical office worker who gives patient data to any unauthorized outside provider of services or supplies. The primary or referring doctor should only authorize services by providers he knows something about.

The Medicare billing system should be changed to avoid anything except necessary medical supplies and services and not allow the billing down to the level of toilet paper and every single item. That asks for "loading the bill". It's really that simple.

**Now we come to insurance.** This has become an ever increasing problem for doctors and patients. The doctors complain about the tons of paperwork work load required of them to get authorizations and processing claims. They are well justified in their complaint but lots can be done through the technology available to make that process paperless. This is simply applying available information technology. The other side is **malpractice and liability insurance.** The mega settlements of millions of Dollars are paid by insurance companies which simply keep jacking up the premiums. A significant part of the settlements go for legal expenses, rather than to the patients who suffered. More and more doctors are leaving private practices joining hospital staffs where they don't have to deal with insurance. That's defrauding patients who need these doctors.

Meanwhile, less people are becoming doctors as that field is becoming less lucrative. All this leads to a crisis in the availability of doctors and ability by people to afford the sky rocketing health insurance premiums. This has placed a big burden on public health across the country creating a pseudo national health system for the poor and uninsured. If you can't afford insurance, you simply go to the county hospital emergency room and **pray you get some service**. At least you know you get some kind of medical care.

The fix to the insurance problem is simple. Reduce the paperwork and limit the malpractice awards with a focus on the huge punitive awards which can cross over $100 million.

Reduced drug costs also can have a significant effect on insurance premiums. Therefore, market forces should be allowed to dictate drug prices rather than being mandated by federal laws.

What's the big deal? There isn't much new here. **The fixes are simple**, are available today and can have a significant beneficial impact. The big deal is that we could do it but don't. The fact that we don't is the **fraud committed by industry and government.**

*A sick health industry has difficulty in helping sick people get better.*
Gunther Karger

# Keep Religion
# Out of Government

*It's God's will. I have been led by God to take this action. We are commanded by God.* Who said these words? A senator in our Congress pressing for a bill passage? Our President justifying an action? An Islamic terrorist about to bomb a train station? The Inquisitor in Spain about 1450? Jim Jones killing over 900 people twenty five years ago? A Roman centurion unleashing his warriors in the name of his God who was Caesar? The high priest wielding his axe sacrificing a young girl to his sun god while his flock cheer him on?

It could be any one or all of the above. They all have much in common. Each is a strong **"believer"** in **his religion.** Each believes that his belief is the only true religion and that his interpretation of what it means is as inflexible as an iron rod. Each believes that he acts in the name of God and is commanded by his God to carry out that task. Any one of these could be Christian, Muslim, Jewish or believer in a faith which sacrifices chickens to gain salvation. Which of the above believes in the right religion? **They all do.**

While most religions have much in common, such as the Ten Commandments, there are many varied interpretations. There are differences between Protestants and Catholics, Lutherans, Methodists, Pentecostals, Mormons, Christian Science, Jewish and more. But there also is much in common between these religions.

There are as significant differences between the Hasidic Jews and conservatives as there are between Sunni Muslims and the Islamic Shiites who have been at war for ages and today wage a bloody civil war against each other in Iraq.

The 30 year war in Northern Europe between 1618 and 1648 was about which religion was best for the country and Europe. Protestant or Catholic? Israeli Prime Minister Rabin was assassinated by an ultra orthodox Jew because he disagreed with his particular interpretation about what the same God wants for Israel.

**Religion is best kept at home, in the church, at bible meetings, churches, temples, mosques and all those places dedicated to the worship of our respective religions.** The business of governing a nation should be about that, leading a nation for the good of all. The founding fathers of America wisely said that our government is for all people and by all people, regardless of race, color or religion and that all shall be free to practice one's own religion without fear or recrimination.

Does this mean that our leaders should or could not be religious or believe strongly in their religions? Absolutely not. In fact, it would be good if our leaders believed in a main stream religion and practiced its principles on a personal basis. However, it is not good for persons of high authority to invoke personal religious beliefs into laws and make decisions based on what *God is telling them to do.* That leads to governments such as exist in Iran where the law of the land is based on religious practices specified by the Shiite brand of Islamic belief. Even Israel has a government ruled by religious law specifying who is Jewish, who is not and who is not Jewish enough to be married by a rabbi.

It's best to keep religion out of government for another good reason. A good leader trying to convince the nation to approve an important program in the national interest lays out the facts in a way the people clearly understand.

When things get unclear and people have difficulty in understanding or agreeing with the leader, a true leader does his best and relies on the will of the people. A poor leader invokes the name of God and tells the people to accept his word because he is a Believer.

He lobbies to the preachers to tell their flock to support their government leader and they should pray for that in the name of their God. They are told that *"you are either for or against me. You should have faith in knowing that God has placed me here and now to lead you through this. If you are against me, you are unpatriotic to our country and unfaithful to God"*. **This is leading by blind belief rather than fact supported logic and can lead to disaster.**

A nation can be deceived into taking the wrong path. Yes, that's why I include the religion dimension within this book about deception and fraud. It **is deception and it is fraudulent** to coerce people into making decisions based on belief rather than fact because such ways tend to **hide information people need to make informed decisions.** This is no different than making financial decisions. We must have facts and base our decisions on them, rather than hope and blind belief. Never forget, When money and power speaks, the whole truth often keeps silent as the flock is steered toward the path of the righteous, that is, the people with the authority of the government.

### *We must work hard to preserve a secular government.*

### *Our children and grand children deserve no less than to inherit a country based on the great principles of America's founding fathers*

# The Economy
# A Reality Check

**Statistics**: a set of data from which nearly any conclusion can be drawn to benefit a predetermined purpose

**What's the real deal with the economy** at the level which means anything to us? The economists and government tells us the economy is doing great while layoffs rise in significant numbers and offshoring accelerates. Although I assess the economy as of mid 2005 prior to Hurricane Katrina, I address what the numbers really mean at any time. It's essential to cut though the economics jargon to get to the meat of all that mumbo jumbo to better help us plan our lives and businesses.

# The U.S. Economy
# What's the Real Deal?

We all want to feel good about the economy because it's about our jobs, income, investments and what we can look forward to in our retirement. When the economists talk, we listen and so does **Wall Street** which goes up and down depending on where the economists tell us the economy is headed. That's important because our investments, pension plans, 401K and IRA accounts are largely invested in Wall Street in either stocks, mutual funds and bonds. Business managers listen to the economists. If the outlook is bright and headed up they expand production and hire more people.

Conversely, if the outlook is bad, they will fire, close plants, reduce production and invest less into new plants and equipment which is generally bad for their suppliers as that has a negative ripple effect. Politicians hate negative forecasts but love good news about the economy because they then take the credit for creating the conditions producing the good performance and that leads to getting elected.

You are right. Nothing new in this. **But are they telling us the real story or just telling us want they know we want to hear to make us feel good?** Are they telling us all that we need to know or leaving out things we should definitely know to give us the balanced picture? This chapter will help you to sort all this out so when you hear the government and economists speak the next time, you can at least know what questions to ask and better understand what they are saying **and what all that means.** We need this knowledge to make better decisions for us personally and for our businesses.

Let's go to June 8 when the White House proudly announced that **"*Economic growth is steady, it is strong at a 3.4% GDP growth and our economy's underlying fundamentals are robust. Further good news is the unemployment rate at a low of 5.2% that we've rarely seen in history and 3.5 million new jobs created over the past two years with an average of 178,000 new jobs per month being added.*"** Before standing up singing hallelujah and praise, let's do a reality check on this great news.

On this very same day, GM announced that it is laying off 25,000 people or about 25% of its entire work force and will close lots of plants. Ford recently announced that it was taking over Visteon Corp. which makes auto parts going into its cars and was about to go under. That company employs about 17,000 many of who may lose their jobs. The auto industry was in a tail spin because of the high fuel costs leading people to dramatically slow down their buying of SUV's and trucks shifting to smaller more fuel efficient vehicles. Suddenly, the auto industry was tooled for the wrong vehicle.

Fuel costs had **soared about 50%** in just a year driven by oil prices nearly doubling to over $55 per barrel. This was principally a result from the much longer than expected Iraq war which as of mid 2005 was continuing with casualties rising instead of falling. This fuel cost increase resulted in an average of about $8 added cost each time you drove to the gas pump and filled your vehicle unless of course you had a Hummer which would have added about $50.

The U.S daily oil consumption of about 20 million barrels per day translates to about $400 million additional cost to the economy for the same oil as a year before. **This is a massive $146 billion sucked right out of the economy in just one year.** Guess what?

This incremental money the country spent went to increase the GDP by that exact amount while doing nothing for the economy because it was paying that extra money for that same oil. If we adjusted the GDP for 2005 to reflect this $146 billion, that would result in a **GDP growth of only 1.03%. That's barely above recession level**. A far cry from the robust 3.4% our politicians and economists told us mid summer, 2005. Then, Hurricane Katrina hit New Orleans and the upper Gulf coast impacting refineries raising oil further to $70 and gasoline over $3 per gallon. If this additional increase were included in these numbers, the economy would look even worse and could slip into a recession.

Worse still, some of the extra $146 billion spent for this same fuel likely came out of other areas of the economy as people and companies have just so much to spend. Just a week before the White House gave this great news, Federal Reserve Chairman Greenspan issued a cautionary statement suggesting that the increased fuel costs may be having a negative impact on the economy and that Fed could soon suspend interest rate increases to rekindle the economy. The airlines are another good example loosing billions and going bankrupt because of the fuel increase. **I would not call this a robust and strong economy even though the White House said it was.** When politicians make statements about the economy, it's a good idea to look around you to see what's actually happening. We need to sort out fact from spin which is a nice word for deception. I refer you to the earlier chapter on "Fraud and Deception.

**Let's move on to the jobs**. The White House statement which incidentally was made by the Secretary of the Treasury said "*our current 5.2% unemployment rate is near the lowest we have seen in history*".

I went to the Bureau of Labor economics statistics published by our government to learn that while the May, 2005 number just then released was 5.2%, down from 6.3% in 2003, the unemployment rate was 3.9% when the Bush administration was first elected in 2000. While the statement that 3.5 million new jobs created was not far off the Bureau of Labor data of about 3 million, **it failed to say that 2.4 million jobs were lost during 2001 and 2002.** This means that a net of only about 600,000 new jobs were created during the present administration. That doesn't include millions of people who dropped off the unemployment rolls as their unemployment compensation either ran out or they got low paying jobs paying much less than the jobs they had lost. This employment data also doesn't reflect the trend toward lower paying service sector jobs as the U.S. economy continues to lose manufacturing to the developing nations. The White House statement says that we are adding an average 178,000 new jobs per month which is correct based on the Bureau of Labor data. **However, it fails to say that we still are laying off an average of 107,000 each month.** Worse still is that the new jobs added tend to be lower paying jobs than the jobs closed out.

I should mention some bright spots in the economy. The **telecom sector is coming back after five years in a deep slump.** The new technologies developed over the past few years are coming to market as telecom operators need to upgrade and expand their networks and the Internet is again showing strong growth.

However, much of this growth is seen in developing nations and underserved areas in the U.S. While much of the development of these new technologies is done in the U.S at places such as Silicon Valley stimulating a strong localized economy, the products they develop are mostly manufactured overseas with well over 50% delivered to foreign customers. Three of the companies we personally invested in during this time frame had more than 90% of their business outside the U.S.

Given all this, how "**robust**" was the economy during this time? **I'll let you judge that for yourself**. I used the data of the time when I wrote this book **to illustrate a point** which remains valid even as the economy changes over time. If I included the impact of Hurricane Katrina, the economy would look even worse. Hopefully, this will turn out to be a short term glitch which will be offset by the massive $200 billion estimated it will take to rebuild the upper Gulf area.

It's very important to properly evaluate the economic numbers as they are issued especially when profound statements are made by politicians. Never forget that their interest is getting elected while your interest is making a living and surviving the ups and downs in any economic climate.

### *Know the difference between spin and reality*

### *Look for the real story instead of just listening to what you want to hear*

# Globalization
# Driven by Technology

**Globalization is here to stay and accelerating**. The best the United States can do is to adopt policies which recognize this new fact of economic life. **Technology is the driver of globalization** focused on advances in transportation and communications.

Globalization in the Western Hemisphere was started by the Viking, **Eric the Red, born about 950 AD** in Norway. When he was 10 years old, Eric was taken to Iceland by his father who was banished by Norway as a murderer. About 985, Eric sailed for Greenland with 25 ships of colonists, but only 14 of the vessels completed the voyage with 450 people.

The settlers farmed the land; raised cattle, hogs, and sheep, hunted bears, caribou and other animals. This was the first leg of globalization **made possible by the strong Viking vessels which could survive the brutal arctic winter storms**. His son Leif Ericsson born 985 AD went west to discover Vinland which later became known as Newfoundland thus discovering North America, about 500 years ahead of Christopher Columbus. The Portugese and Spaniards extended globalization using more advances in ship design and stellar navigation. That enabled Columbus to reach America in 1490 and made it possible for Ferdinand Magellan to circumnavigate the globe in 1519.

Magellan established trading with the East Indies leading Manila to become the greatest commerce center of that region providing spices for the world. We should view this Asian trade as the beginning of globalization of commerce taking place nearly 900 years before China and India became a threat to American commerce.

This was made possible by Columbus learning from the works of ancient Greek astronomers who studied the heavens in the years around 141 AD. They described the relationship between the earth and the stars which helped Columbus to use the sextant which is a mechanical device telling the navigator the ship's location.

**The Industrial Revolution** started in the mid 1700's in England by applying power to agriculture and some industries using the steam engine invented by James Watt in 1769. The first boat assisted by **steam engine** was the Savannah which sailed in 1819 from New York to Liverpool in 29 days. As an aside, in 1946 I emigrated to the United States at age 13 as a war orphan sailing on the SS Gripsholm from Sweden via Liverpool to New York. That took only 14 days. This marriage between industrial production and advances in shipping **triggered the next wave of globalization** resulting in mass production and shipping speed.

Michael Faraday became the next significant contributor in globalization by inventing the **electric motor** in 1831. He was followed by Nikola Tesla who is the original inventor of **radio communications** resulting from his experimentation with magnetic fields and electric currents.

While he was granted the original patent for radio, it was Guglielmo Marconi who was first to successfully transmit his telegraph signal across the Atlantic in 1902. From a globalization view, this was more important than Alexander Graham Bell's inventing the telephone earlier in 1876 as that required wires. The Industrial revolution began to accelerate when Thomas Edison invented the first practical **light bulb** in 1879 although I should mention that it was Humphry Davy, the English chemist who was the original inventor of the light bulb much earlier in 1809.

The early driving force to industrial and globalization was the **ability to produce** products and the **speed by which they were transported.** This process accelerated with the airplane which enabled people and goods to be shipped across continents and oceans in hours instead of weeks.

The next leap into accelerated globalization and in fact reaching beyond into space was the **invention of the transistor,** often called one of the most important technological events of the 20th Century. This is credited to John Bardeen, Walter Brattain and William Shockley who discovered that dramatic amplification could be achieved using solid materials such as silicon and germanium instead of the bulky and power hungry vacuum tube.

These scientists worked at the Bell Telephone Laboratories in New Jersey where I also was a research scientist developing products for communications and computer storage. The transistor reduced the size of electronic components to eventually the current extremely small microchip we now have in nearly everything we know today. William Shockley is the person who brought the silicon to Silicon Valley and started that entire industry.

The next wave toward globalization was the development of high **speed communications** via fiber optic cables, satellites and other forms of wireless systems. This is what enabled the Internet to evolve over just the past ten years and what made it possible for under developed areas of the world to join the world's **second generation of the Industrial Revolution.**

This is what enables you to pick up your cellular telephone while driving your car ordering a computer made in China and delivered to your door steps within 24 hours charged to your bank account before you get to your destination. Today, we are well on the way of becoming a global society because **technology brought us closer together via transportation, communications and politics.**

The fall of the Soviet Union in 1991 heralded in a massive long term world economic growth resulting from the adoption of a free capitalist society by a vast part of the world's population. Although still governed by a communist regime, China with its 1.3 billion people has become a major world economic force with India and its 1 billion not far behind. The European Union has been evolving into a single economic force now using a common currency with trade barriers between the countries mostly removed.

**This is an irreversible and accelerating global trend the United States must recognize, accept and make the most of**. Rather than seeking isolation which appears to be the policy of the present administration, the United States must adopt policy demonstrating leadership and cooperation to foster economic growth among all the nations.

## *"Together we thrive, apart we fall"*
Gunther Karger

# Definition of Globalization

Edited by Shirley Karger

**Question**: What is the best definition of **globalization?**
**Answer: Princess Diana**
**Question: Why Princess Diana?**

She was an **English** princess with an **Egyptian** boyfriend, who crashed into a **French** tunnel, driving a **German** car with a **Dutch** engine driven by a **Belgian** driver who was drunk on **Scottish** whisky, followed closely by **Italian** paparazzi on a **Japanese** motorcycle, treated by an **American** doctor who used **Brazilian** medicines.

This is sent to you by an **American** using Bill Gates **technology** and you probably are reading this on your computer which uses **Taiwanese chips** and a **Korean monitor** which was assembled by **Bangladeshi workers** in a **Singapore plant**, transported by **Indian truck** drivers and hijacked by **Indonesians** and unloaded by **Sicilian longshoremen** and finally trucked to you by **Mexican illegals.**

*The essence of the above was found on an "Internet quip"*
*edited by Shirley Karger into the above "little story"*

# Outsourcing-Offshoring
# Here to Stay

When we think of outsourcing, we too often think about loss of jobs in the United States to other countries driving up our unemployment and depressing our economy. First, let's define what we are talking about.

**Outsourcing** is hiring a maid to clean your house, your gardener to cut your lawn, your plumber to fix your plugged toilet and your accountant doing your taxes. Instead of you doing these tasks, you let someone else do them. Could you do them? Maybe yes, but you would first have to learn how to do them efficiently and invest in the right tools. Instead of you spending your time and money investing in tools and training, you focus on your job making your primary living. Then, you take some of the money you make in that job and pay someone else to do these tasks.

Business does the same thing. Your employer contracts with a food service company to operate the cafeteria in your office building. Boeing contracts Motorola to make the communications equipment for the aircraft instead of having it's own electronics department doing that. Macy's department store hires an outside security firm to prevent shoplifting instead of having its own security force. **This is outsourcing.** It's as old as history itself and is worldwide.

**Offshoring** is relatively new made possible in recent years by dramatic technological breakthroughs and political changes. Large cargo aircraft, high speed communications and countries cooperating in friendly political relations made it possible for a product to be designed in the United States, manufactured in China and be delivered to nearly any place in the world within 48 hours.

When you pick up your phone to make an airline reservation on Delta Airlines, you likely will reach an agent in India where Delta has a reservations center staffed by Indian people. Likewise, if you have a question about your credit card statement, when you call that toll free 800 number, you also will likely reach someone in India or another country. **That's offshoring** and it's an extension of outsourcing using personnel resources outside your country using modern technology and enabling friendlier political and economic systems of other nations.

Offshoring is an extension of international commerce. GM announced in early June 2005 that it would lay off 25,000 people and close some manufacturing plants in the U.S. This reflected recommendations by its advisers that it should close several major vehicle assembly plants in the U.S capable of producing 1 million cars annually and be replaced by assembly plants in China exporting 300,000 vehicles per year to the U.S. by 2007. This is an example of offshoring manufacturing but it's not a new thing. The U.S. textile and shoe industry has all but been totally offshored. No TV is today being produced in the U.S. nor are most of consumer electronics.

More recently, resulting from the emergence of the Internet, availability of high speed data communications and the now evolving Voice over Internet(VoIP), call center operations have been largely offshored with the more high tech information technology support operations (IT) following closely on its heels. India with it's 1 billion people and a large English speaking population by 2005 had 1 million people working call centers and doing related "offshoring" tasks for clients all over the world but principally in the U.S. Meeting the needs of this growing industry serving countries other than the U.S., India plans to hire 120,000 non English speaking employees speaking German, Spanish and other European languages.

India's outsourcing business grew 35% in 2005 from $12 billion to $17 billion and is expected to reach $50 billion by 2009. General Electric started an "**offshoring call center**" business in India which by 2004 employed 12,000 people to serve its own corporate needs and which GE eventually sold for $400 million.

India is not the only country focused on supplying the world's outsourcing needs with cheap labor made possible by its 1 billion population. China has made a dramatic impact on world commerce and in particular on the U.S. which I will discuss in a separate chapter.

**Offshoring** is not a temporary phenomenon. It's here to stay and probably will accelerate. The best we in America can and should do is to adopt commerce and political policies **encouraging international cooperation and retool ourselves** to take advantage of this trend. It's vitally important that we better understand this to offset propaganda and misleading information too often seen given by our leaders and commentators. If a politician tells us to vote for him because he will bring the jobs back, he is giving an unrealistic expectation, is telling us what we want to hear but we should not vote for him. But if a politician acknowledges globalization as an evolutionary trend and gives us a plan how we can better fit and grow within that new world, he is telling the truth and may be worth voting for. **We need to separate fact from spin.**

# Here Comes China

*"There lies a sleeping giant. Let him sleep because when he wakes he will shake the entire world"*
Napoleon Bonaparte, 1803

President Bush's foreign post 9/11 policy was to bring democracy to the far corners of the world because people in a free society will flourish. As this book is written, a fierce war already into its third year is raging in Iraq to bring this "message" to a people who never lived in a democracy. The message we are telling the world is that a free Iraq will become a beacon to the entire Mid East thus resolving the terrorism problem.

**History does not support such a policy.** The Shah of Iran modernized his country using Western style methods bringing industry and to some extent liberated women and intellectuals. **Still, he was an absolute ruler.** When the insurgents rose to the call of liberation of Iran from this **"tyrant"**, President Jimmy Carter stood aside in the name of human rights rather than help preserve the government which was a friend of the West. The Ayatollah Khomeini and his Islamic legions succeeded in overthrowing the Shah's regime. Following the Shah came a regime far more oppressive and brutal. That regime was based on the laws of fundamentalist Islam which basically declared war on the "West" starting with the storming of the U.S. embassy and holding hostages for over a year. Since then, Iran has became the beacon of Islamic fundamentalism which helped create the Taliban in Afghanistan and support the Hamas who lead terrorism in Israel. Today, a young group of Islamic fundamentalists have taken over from the Ayatollahs and present the West with a nuclear threat while supporting freed Iraqi Shiites with modern weapons which at some future time may be used against the U.S. and the West.

That happened in Afghanistan where the U.S. supported Osama bin Laden and his Taliban friends to get rid of the Soviets. Today, the Russians (former Soviets) are our friends and Osama bin Laden is our arch enemy. If today, in 2005, an election were held in Saudi Arabia following the death of King Fahd and Osama bin Laden were running for the new King, Osama bin Laden, also a Saudi, would likely be elected taking that country backwards just as happened in Iran when the Shah was dethroned. The U.S. administration strongly supports the ruling Saudi regime which is no more than an absolute dictator in the guise of a king and his royal family and that's not a democracy.

Yugoslavia under dictator Tito flourished economically for 50 years until his death when that entire area crumbled politically and economically. The Balkans splintered demographically and geographically between ethic groups as the area grappled with democracy. The West had to come in to stop ethnic cleansing and mass killings reminiscent of the Hitlerian days. Monaco is an example where one ruler, the prince, is in absolute control over this tiny country which has economically flourished since its beginning as a gambling mecca on the French Riviera.

**Here comes China** which remains without a question a country ruled by the communist party called the Peoples Republic of China (PRC). Mao Tse Tung, who led the revolution of 1949 established the PRC and gave the world his famous words in his little red book "Quotations from Chairman Mao *"Dare to struggle and dare to win"*. Despite the long lasting oppressive regime of Mao and his successors who supported the Korean War, Vietnam and the Tiananmen massacre in 1989 and the United States still talking about trade sanctions to punish China, it has grown to be the world's second largest economic force. The U.S in 2004 was China's largest export partner with $134 billion representing 23% of its $583 billion total exports.

There is no doubt that China's cheap exports contribute materially to the low inflation seen in recent years in the U.S. assisted by investments by the Chinese into U.S. industries and companies. Under the communist rule still in place in China, more and more private capitalists are flourishing. The Lenovo Group headed by a 40 year old Chinese computer engineer just bought out IBM's PC business for $1.25 billion creating a world computer powerhouse of $12 billion in sales with HQ in New York and principal operations in Bejing and North Carolina. China is expected to surpass Nokia in 2006 as the world's largest cell phone manufacturer, already in 2005 has an estimated 300 million cell phone users and growing rapidly. China's largest online entertainment company was founded by a 34 year old computer engineer and today has 300 million subscribers including an online gaming business.

Today, in 2005, China's gross domestic product stands at $7.3 trillion growing at 9.3% compared with the U.S GDP at $11.7 trillion growing at 3.5%. The Chinese economy is driven by an abundant supply of labor fueled by 1.3 billion people with unemployment in the urban areas still a high 9.8% and overall country unemployment at about 20%. The economy is technologically driven with a highly educated work force produced by universities all over China. The nation's rulers including the president and every cabinet level minister is an engineering graduate. Despite the communist regime still in place and censorship of the Chinese Internet about to significantly increase, how can anyone say that China is not flourishing?

China is definitely not a democratic nation. **Yet, the present administration insists democracy is a prerequisite to economic growth of a nation and a region.** Chairman Mao's famous words of a half century ago appear to have been prophetic when he told his masses **"Dare to struggle and dare to win".** China struggled and became great relative to the world despite maintaining the same basic form of regime.

**What's the lesson of this chapter in context with this book on fraud and deception?** We need to maintain an open view and see through the window of truth about what the world is as it really exists. We must recognize propaganda and judge for ourselves how the United States is evolving relative to the rest of the world.

This helps us realize that all areas of the world regardless of what kind of regime or ethnic focus can have vastly different cultures representing thousand of years of history and still flourish. We must all be willing to adjust to the reality of change as technology brings the 6 billion people of the world closer together. We must also learn to better coexist while recognizing and respecting our root differences. Failure to do otherwise results in isolation and domestic economic stagnation. We must take the best of what exists in each nation and learn to work together instead of trying to change each other's cultures.

## *Cooperation is better than confrontation.*

# Investment Strategy For the Future

**Unless you send out a ship, you won't catch any fish.** But you must know where the best fish are and constantly watch out for storms, tsunamis and pirates. You also should avoid cesspools where you'll likely snare dead fish which ruin your good catch already caught.

**As we near the end of this book**, we have come through a lot of storms, turbulent waters and observed that these conditions have been with us since the beginning of time. We even bridged the time warp of 3500 years from ancient Troy to modern Enron and examined Carlo Ponzi's journey which took him all over the United States and ended in Brazil 50 years later. Our daily news gives us what seems to be a bottomless barrel of rotten eggs from the business world which the current reformers address.

**We recall the "Teapot Dome"** oil scandal of the 1920's when President Harding's Secretary of the Interior was receiving huge bribes from his oil friends by awarding them leases at our nation's strategic oil reserves one of which was called "Tea Pot Dome". Today, we have the **sudden rise in oil prices from $30 to $70** with oil producers making billions in sudden new profit lining sheikdoms in oil rich Arabia and bringing a pot of gold to the oil service companies based mostly in Texas.

How can we forget **Rudy Guiliani** in the 80's when he was the U.S. Prosecutor in New York clearing such folk as Michael Milken and Ivan Boesky out of the investment barrel leading him to be later the illustrious Mayor of New York to lead that metropolis through its 9/11 disaster?

Today, we have **Eliot Spitzer**, New York State's Attorney General going after entire industries such as mutual funds and insurance cleaning out huge conflicts of interest paid for by you and I across the country. He is doing the work the SEC in Washington should have been doing and as I write this book, he is eying the New York Governor's house. Maybe we'll be lucky and he might someday move south to Washington to occupy a white house.

So, armed with the tidbits from this book, we now can continue our journey and invest because what else could we do with our money? **After all, there are many honest folks out there, just like you.** Penalties for misdeeds have risen. Bernie Ebbers got a 25 years prison term and he lost his entire fortune compared with Michael Milken who served only 22 months and walked out of prison with a $700 million fortune even after paying $600 million in fines when he entered the portal of jail. One thing is for sure, as the companies and deals get bigger with each generation, so do also the risks and rewards. It's the old proverb from tales of Arabia as I put right up front in this book " **An egg thief becomes a camel thief**". We just have to learn along with them and work a little harder and smarter to stay ahead of them.

**So what do we do now** and in future years? This book will last as long as **Thieves on Wall Street** which still today is as valid as it was ten years ago when I wrote it. Although considered a maverick and occasionally laughed at, even after appearing on the nationally televised CNN Money Show, most of what I said in that book did happen and turned out prophetic as we have seen during the past few years.

It's simple. We just move on and apply sound investment principles and common sense as we always should have done but occasionally failed because things got too easy and the **fever of greed** came along. When things seem too good to be true, we should pause and take a second look before taking that leap.

**We should focus on companies** with real revenues and products. Technology has always been an exciting area as our civilization accelerates driven by new products and services. Just 20 years ago, personal computers were a novelty and cellular telephones were an expensive business tool ten years ago. Two years ago, when you went to the clinic for an x-ray, you had to wait days for the results and two weeks for an appointment with the doctor to tell give you the good or bad news. Today, you go to a neighborhood diagnostic center where in less than one hour your x-ray is taken and digitally transmitted to a radiology specialist who while you wait sends the report via high speed communications to you before you leave that center.

Less than five years ago, you paid your bills by writing out a check and licking stamps to the envelope and took it to the mailbox hoping that the mail system would deliver your payment by the due date. Today, you get on your computer and with a few simple keystrokes, you transfer the payment from your checking account to the payee. Five years ago, you paid $3,000 for an average home computer still out of reach for many. Today, you can buy a much faster computer doing more for less than $500 and a printer comes with it. By 2006, you can use your handheld PDA and do much of what you today do on your home and notebook computer while you are on the move, just like a cellular telephone. Already today, you can look up your investments, trade your stocks and get emails on your small wireless handheld device. Of course, you have done so already on your PC during just the past few years.

**Technology is what's rapidly changing our world to make it better and this is a global trend**. Although the developed nations have only about a billion population, the rest of the world is growing and improving and that's an additional 5 billion people.

Although China with its 1.3 billion people and India trailing just behind with 1 billion are making significant contributions to world trade, the rest of the world is rising. While parts of Africa seem destitute as are countries such as Bangladesh, Peru and others, more and more countries are implementing infrastructures based on the evolving latest technologies. Communities high in the Andes in South America are seeing some industrialization with more jobs made possible by connecting them via satellite communications and short takeoff and landing aircraft.

China's urgent need for increased electrification in its rural areas is being increasingly met by wind energy. The outdated and often non existent communications infrastructures of Eastern Europe, Central Asia, Southeast Asia and Africa are being replaced by modern wireless high speed communications networks. Five years ago, a small California based technology company developed and installed a satellite based telemedicine system linking hospitals and clinics all across China using a satellite communications network. A U.S. based company installed a satellite based communications network linking bank branches and ATM's all across central Africa.

**Communications and information technology** have been and will continue to be the driving force of economies throughout the world. Although we have seen America slip over the past several years and we have addressed these trends in this book, we must focus on the global economy, rather than just here in the United States.

Although we will see growth in our country, it will be less than the rest of the world and that's why our investment view should be global. **A good investment policy to follow** is to invest in a public company trading on either the New York Stock Exchange or the NASDAQ with at least 51% of its products and services sold in foreign markets. It doesn't matter whether the company is based in the United States or elsewhere so long as it trades on an exchange regulated by the SEC and under the rules of the NYSE and NASDAQ.

This gives us uniformity in some protection and access to required public disclosures which have been made very easy thanks to the Internet modern communications. **Modern communications and new regulations** make it possible for an individual investor to receive press releases via email, participate on corporate conference calls or simply view such presentations on your computer via the rising number of webcasts. The very technologies we should invest in are the ones we can use to track our own investments and this is getting easier and more efficient each year. You can get this information whether you are home in front of your computer, taking a stroll using your cell phone or wireless enabled PDA or even while fishing on a small boat and yes, on a cruise ship off the coast of South America.

When we go on our cruises giving lectures about what's in this book, I daily check my investments and e-mails using the ship's computer which give internet access via a satellite network. This past December, while on a cruise to South America, I received an emailed press release about one of the companies we had stock in and the news was bad. I immediately, right there and then on that computer on the ship off the coast of South America, accessed our own online brokerage firm and sold a significant amount of the stock in that company to protect our assets. When we returned, I sold the rest after a more thorough analysis.

**Yes, we always face risks in investments** and I have addressed some of these risks in this book to help you avoid them. On the following page are a few guidelines in further limiting the risks while maximizing investment gains over the years.

# Investment Guidelines

- Avoid startups and small companies with little or no revenues and unseasoned management.
- Gain at least a minimum understanding of the products and technology offered by the company and maintain awareness of trends to avoid holding stock in companies with mature or declining product demand or unresolved continuing management problems.
- Invest only in financially strong companies with cash on hand of at least 50% of revenues if less than $100 million in annual revenues and 25% if greater. That gives adequate resource for new growth and protects against occasional unforeseen temporary setbacks.
- Avoid companies which have concentration of product sales in any one country using the rule that at least 51% of all products and services sold should be outside the United States distributed over many countries. One of the companies in which we at this time maintain investment is headquartered in the United States, has development and manufacturing in England and Israel and sells to 100 countries and has been in business for nearly 15 years.
- Regularly check the SEC filings for "insider selling" of stock. If there is steady selling by several insiders such as board members, CEO and CFO, seriously consider selling your stock or at least half of it. They know what you don't know but you don't yet know what it is. It's best to limit your exposure and risk in such cases.
- Be aggressive about contacting the company with your concerns. Insist on answers and sell if you think you get less than honest answers.

**A word about real estate investments.** Over the past few years, real estate has risen in value considerably and been a good investment for many. As the stock market slumped for years following the Internet bust and Telecom meltdown, investors shifted their money from stock to real estate. Adding to the rise in value the past two years is the depreciated Dollar principally vs the Euro. This means that a person with Euros buying real estate in the U.S. gets about a 30% discount on whatever he buys relative to what you and I buy.

While real estate will always be a good long term investment depending on location, it is subject to corrections and occasional long periods of stagnation to digest earlier rapid rises. I believe we today, in 2005, are in a period where we will likely face a slowing rise and possibly even some stagnation depending on where the real estate is located. For example, in South Florida which has seen a dramatic rise in values over the past three years, the values are today so high that they are beyond the means of renters and many investors depend on rents covering the rising expenses such as taxes and hurricane insurance. This leads to a word of caution relative to the situation as I see it in the 2005-06 time frame.

**Real estate is a relatively illiquid investment**. This means that you may not be able to quickly sell if you have a personal financial crisis dictating that you raise quick cash. It usually takes at least two months to sell and can take more than six months unless you sell in a crisis sale. In contrast to real estate, we can sell stocks and get cash in three business days and the decision is as quick as your telephone or one keystroke on your computer. **As we get older, we should have less illiquid investments** so that we have access to living funds during our senior years.

**Armed with the insight given in this book** and the information now so readily and easily available, you should without hesitation continue to invest. **Never forget that unless you send the ship out, it will never reach that port.**

Now, my friends, I leave you with these final words:

*"As we set sail on our journey, we must know wind and current, before we can reach distant shore.*

*We must prepare for storm and be vigilant against serpent and pirate.*

*We must set our destination and know when we have arrived, to enjoy the harvest from our crossing."*

**Gunther Karger – 2005**

# References

The information in this book is based on official data wherever possible such as the U.S. Government Bureau of Labor Statistical databases. Information on foreign countries is derived from the latest online CIA Fact Book. We derive information and data from special reports in the Wall Street Journal, the wire services such as Reuters and Dow Jones News and focus reports in prominent publications. For example, we derived information on China from a special report on China in the IEEE Spectrum which is the official magazine of the Institute of Electrical and Electronics Engineers of which I am Senior Life Member and is the world's largest professional organization of electrical engineers. Economic forecasts referred to are derived from the quarterly survey of the 40 leading economists published quarterly in the Wall Street Journal. We make frequent use of news releases about legal matters and go directly to official court records of the U.S. Court System such as PACER(Public Access Court Electronic Records). Projections and estimates are either derived from the above referenced sources or prepared by myself but in each case, they are based on official historical records such as referenced above.

The information presented in this book is current as of the time of its writing which is summer of 2005 and is subject to change due to occasional historical revisions. I have made the best possible effort in presenting accurate historical data but cannot guarantee it.

**The purpose of this book is not to present data. It is to present fresh analysis and unbiased conclusions based on the most recent  best data available.**

# Gunther and Shirley Karger

Gunther & Shirley Karger are shown together because without the support and active help from his wife of 51 years, this book and its related work over the years would not have been possible. They worked side by side creating this book as they did "*Thieves on Wall Street*". While Gunther lectured onboard major cruise lines such as Celebrity Cruises and Radisson Seven Seas and at universities, Shirley assisted during the interactive part of the sessions. Shirley edited this book, his previous book and all the reports issued worldwide via emails and was in charge of marketing and distribution of the "Discovery Letter" published for nearly 20 years. During the Cold War and the Space Program, Shirley was Gunther's official hostess while he served as Chairman of the Institute of Electrical and Electronics Engineers at Cape Canaveral and in New Jersey. They always were and remain a team.

# Gunther Karger

Gunther Karger's career include electronics engineering, corporate management, investment research, stock brokerage, investigative reporting and publishing a stock newsletter. As a technologist, he worked at Bell Telephone Laboratories, Boeing and ITT Communications Systems developing communications networks and aerospace systems for military and intelligence. He was Project Manager of Strategic Command Control Systems during the Cold War as part of a high level team working for the Secretary of Defense. He served as director of strategic planning for major corporations responsible for economic planning and forecasting. He left the corporate world in 1987 to found Discovery Group focused on specialized investment research, fraud investigations and public policy. Karger is author of *"Thieves on Wall Street"*, columnist and published the Discovery Letter which was nationally circulated for 20 years. He frequently speaks on major cruise lines, at universities and private functions and has appeared on network TV including CNN and CNBC. He has served on a number of national boards on Holocaust reparation matters. Gunther Karger is NASD Arbitrator settling financial disputes between the brokerage industry and investors.

Karger, born 1933 in Germany's Black Forest, was sent at age 6 to Sweden in 1939 to survive World War II and the Holocaust. He is a sole survivor of his family who perished in European concentration camps. Karger was raised in foster homes and orphanages in Sweden and the U.S. He served in the U.S. Air Force during the Korean War as an aviation electronics instructor, graduated Louisiana State University in electrical engineering, served as Chairman of the Institute of Electrical and Electronics Engineers at Cape Canaveral in the 60's and was named Outstanding Young Man of America by the U.S. Jaycees in 1965. Gunther and his wife, Shirley live in Palmetto Bay, Florida where he is active in local civic and political roles. The Kargers have two grown sons.

# Contact Information

**Gunther Karger** may be contacted preferably via email at **Gunther@ieee.org** or 305-378-0311

**Books may be ordered** directly by going to his website at **www.guntherkarger.com** which has a secure area processing credit card purchases

**Gunther Karger is available for speaking engagements and consulting assignments.**